I0481119

THE INNOVATIVE THINKING BIBLE
Cracking The Creative Code!

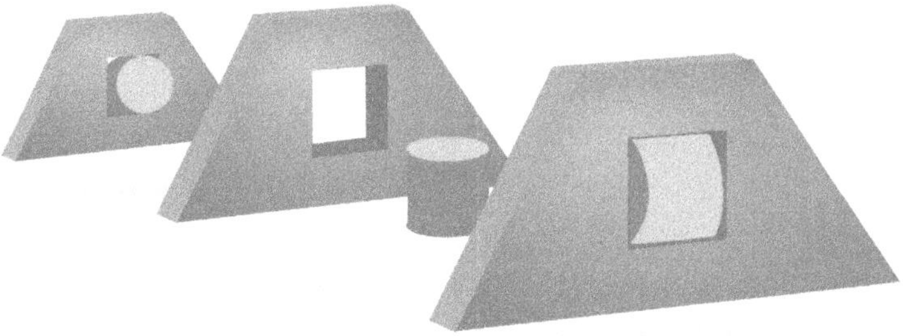

Lon Safko
"An American Innovator"

Printed in the United States of America

This book was created using 100% recycled electrons

No animals were harmed in the making of this book

This Book is Dolphin Safe

Batteries Not Included

Mileage May Vary

Hormone Free

Free Range

Table of Contents

ACKNOWLEDGMENTS

I would like to thank ~~the academy~~ all of the scientists, psychologists, psychiatrists, therapists, crazies, and human Guinea pigs for creating all these invaluable studies, illusions, tests, and observations. For without their work, well the book would have been only a dozen pages.

Also, a big thank you goes out to Steve Wright for being so innovative and looking at the world in a way that makes the rest of us laugh.

And thank you Sir Isaac Newton for ~~stealing, borrowing,~~ being inspired in 1675 when he said: "If I have seen further it is by standing on the shoulders of Giants." And, later 1962 when Francis Crick used the quote in his acceptance speech for winning the Nobel Peace Prize in Physiology or Medicine.

So, I will say… What they said!

Testimonials

"Lon has pulled off a real trick, teaching readers how to be more creative while keeping them completely entertained at the same time! His breezy style, dozens of examples, and fun exercises make this a great book for anyone who wants to be more creative or any organization wanting more creative employees."

- Dr. Gary Witt, Ph.D., Psychological Marketing, L.L.C.

"The Innovative Thinking Bible inspires me to want to invent. You challenge the reader to be creative, to learn from others' mistakes and to innovate at the right time. I've been an innovator and professor for many years, and I know you will change lives with this new book."

- Dr. Mary Beth McCabe, National University

"One of the reasons Lon has been such a successful innovator is because he has always embraced creativity. If creativity does not come as naturally to you, this is the book you need to develop it! Filled with tips, exercises, stories, and quotes, Cracking the Creativity code is just what you need to ignite your creativity."

- Diane Hamilton, Ph.D., Nationally Syndicated Radio Business Show Host

"Caution: Lon Safko's ideas and energy can be contagious. Lon defies categories. He thinks out of a traditional box, bounds, or book. Lon is both wise and witty, cosmic and comic. While Lon has many credits, he does not rest on history. He is about what's next."

- Natalie Butto, Ph.D., Professor, Presenter, Facilitator
Travel Planners International Affiliate

Introduction

This book is innovative, creative, and unlike any book, you have ever read. It will have Fortune 500 examples of creative and innovative success and catastrophic failure. I describe dozens of my own success and failure stories, both of which were on an epic scale. Innovation and creativity aren't only about successes. You learn far more by your failures than you can ever learn from your successes.

This book also contains dozens of insightful personal quotes I have learned from the "school of hard knocks". By understanding these examples you can identify a list of monumental mistakes of you can avoid.

There are dozens of personal examples of innovative successes I have created over the past 30+ years. In addition, there and many great ideas from other individuals whose names are synonymous with the names of Fortune 500 companies such as, Ford, Firestone, and Gillette.

I am sure there will be some reader that might complain about how many personal experiences and ideas I share with you, but that how the process works. I lived these innovative thoughts. I will share as much personal experience and process with you as I can possibly share. If you think it is obsessive, simply skip over as many as you wish.

There are be dozens of sound bytes from one of the most innovative comedian I have ever heard, Steven Wright. I met Steven in 1996 and realized his brain worked similarly to my own. It is his ability to associate unassociated objects that made his humor funny. He just looked at everything… Differently.

Inserting comedy sound bytes in a book isn't an easy feat, but after writing The Social Media Bible, published by John Wiley & Sons, I realized you can connect the virtual world with the world of paper; through QR Barcodes or Quick Response Bar Codes. If you are reading this in an "e" format, URL links to any sound file, video file, PDF, or web link you will need is provided. Simply by "touching" the link, you can view / hear the additional information.

If you are reading this book printed on paper, accessing the additional information is very easy. You will need to download one of the many QR Barcode readers. No matter what platform your smartphone or tablet you have, there are free Barcode readers for you! All you do is download it one, tap to open the app, then use your camera to look at the barcode, and once the camera focuses, you will be taken to the information.

If you've never used a QR Barcode reader, please don't worry about it. It really is very easy to use and it's fun!

You also have the opportunity to participate in more than 40 exercises which will reinforce what we discussed. This will help you to better understand and more easily repeat that exercises allowing you to build your brain like a muscle. The brain needs exercise, only we call it practice.

Also, I will put information I wasn't able to put in this book on my website. Just go to www.Safko.com, select "Free Content Access" and I will send you a password to access all the free content in this book.

If you were to learn to play golf, ride a bike, or play the piano, all of these activities would require you to practice the drill or exercise. This practice builds neurons and connects pathways between neurons that will simply make you better at performing these types of tasks.

The materials in this book are the latest, most cutting-edge information available today showing us how our brains think, innovate, and create. I have been studying these processes for more than two decades, while actually practicing them for the more than six decades I have been around and… thinking.

I have been gathering the contents of this book for nearly two decades. While most of the concepts are original, many of the tests, quotes, and illusions have been around for a long time being used by psychologists and other scientists. If I included anything that I should have given credit to, please let me know and I will give credit where credit is due. If I included anything that the rightful owner would like to see removed, it will be removed immediately upon notice.

Also, each complete thought will be separated as an individual page(s), eliminating run-on sentences and run on chapters. Every page or two is set up as a logical stopping point. Read the thought, go onto another thought, or simply take a break. You aren't required to reread what you previously read unless you want to.

This was an innovative way to keep up with the times, the trends, and how people are now reading books.

In May of 2015, Time Magazine published an article about a study performed by Microsoft about the new, human attention span. For the very first time ever, the human attention span tested lower (shorter) than that of a goldfish. Yes, a goldfish has a longer attention span than do we. **http://ti.me/1A2jCJd**

The study showed in the year 2000, the goldfish tested with an attention span of 9 seconds, while humans tested out at 12. The test was then performed again in 2013 and while the goldfish maintained their 9 second span, we humans dropped to 8 seconds falling below that of the goldfish. This has a significant effect on how we communicate, market, support.

We no longer can find the time to read a book, or do we have time for a shorter eBook. A white paper is now too time-consuming. Even a 10 minute video is closed out of by the third minute.

Enjoy learning all these amazing techniques and most importantly, benefit from them. There is one caveat though, you have to be committed. You have to make a commitment to yourself that you will do the exercises, work out the problems, read and understand the quotes and stories. The more you commit, the more time you spend practicing the information this book, the better you will become at Innovative Thinking and the more reward you will get from the time you've spent sharing these ideas.

If you would like to learn more, please visit www.Safko.com.

Drop me a note and share your experiences, your successes, your failures, or if you simply have a question for me, you can email me at lon@Safko.com.

Please go, learn, enjoy, and benefit!

Lon Safko, your author…

About The Author

Let's set the stage right up front. In case you were wondering if I have actually been there, done that, and had earned the right to call myself an "innovation expert", I wanted to provide at least some of the innovative accomplishments I have achieved over the past several decades. You don't need to read them all, just scan them until you are convinced.

- Star of the PBS Television Special "Social Media & You... Communicating In A Digital World".
- Invented the "First Computer To Save A Human Life".
- 18 Inventions & 30,000 personal records in the Smithsonian Institution, Washington, D.C.
- Spent most of my career as an entrepreneur, innovator, president, and CEO.
- An innovator for more four decades founding 14 start-up companies.
- Invented the first voice recognition and the first home automation for the disabled.
- Invented the first three-dimensional virtual environment.
- Invented the first integrated computer system for the physically disabled.
- Invented the archetype of Apple Newton and Microsoft's Bob operating systems.
- Invented "Tool-Tips", and first software user 's guides.
- Has 14 Inventions in the Computer History Museum, Mountainview, CA
- Awarded 3 patents on three-dimensional Internet advertising and "Virtual-Electronic-Retailing"
- Awarded 125 software copyrights, trademarks, a dozen signature marks.
- Recipient of The Westinghouse Entrepreneur of the Year Award.
- Recipient of The Arizona Software Association's Entrepreneur of the Year Award.

- Recipient of The the Arizona Innovation Network's Innovator of the Year Award.
- Recipient of The Public Relations Society of America's "Mark of Excellence" Award.
- Recipient of The A.A.P.A.'s Award of Excellence for the Western Hemisphere.
- Twice nominated Entrepreneur of the Year by Ernst & Young / Inc. Magazine.
- Recognized by the Department of Veteran's Affairs and the Phoenix Mayor's Council.
- Featured in Entrepreneur Magazine, Inc. Magazine, PC Novice, Popular Science, & NY Times.
- Appointed USA Today CEO Advisory Board, the first SCORE Ambassador.
- Author of the bestselling book "The Social Media Bible", Third Edition, hit #1 on Amazon, exceeded $2m in sales
- Author of the bestselling book "The Fusion Marketing Bible", hit #3 on Amazon & the concept is Patent Pending!
- Author of the bestselling book "Innovative Thinking, Cracking The Creativity Code".
- Nominated for a Pulitzer Prize & Member of MENSA.

Expectations

As I stated in the Introduction, creativity and Innovation is a skill, it's not a talent. Everyone can learn to play piano, ride a bicycle, & and play golf. While we all can learn to play, some people will still be "naturals", people who were born with the talent and ability already formed in their brains and required less practice than the rest of us to become great.

With practice, you can become good, very good, and possibly great at thinking more creatively. You might not become the next Amadeus Mozart, Michelangelo, or Jack Nicklaus, but maybe that's OK too as long as you can think creatively and solve problems better than you did. And I promise, if you practice, solving problems, developing new ideas, inventing new products, finding new markets for your existing products, or just having fun, you will become more innovative!

You are going to learn the rules, what to do, what not to do, and how to do it better. You'll see how to perform a certain task and then you'll be ask to perform that task yourself. You will be given methods for understanding how and why it works. You will have the opportunity to participate in more than 40 individual and team Activities.

Provided are 100's of genius quotes, videos, stories, and examples of how people have succeeded by doing what was taught in this book.

The rest is up to you… Only you can do the work. This book can just be entertaining by reading other successes and failures or if you just want to have fun doing the exercises, then this book is also for you. If you take innovative thinking seriously and want to outperform your competition and simply be more creative, then you will have to do the work. You will have to make a commitment to putting the effort into practicing the activities, studying the examples, and creating the environment necessary to achieve your goals. So, the big question is…

Are you committed? If so, let's go!

CHAPTER 1

PERSPECTCVE

Chapter 1

PERSPECIVE

Creativity Isn't A Talent

It's important enough to wash, rinse, repeat. Creativity is a learned process, just like riding a bike, playing golf, or playing the piano. the more you practice the quicker you will become an expert at being innovative.

Just like any sport, musical instrument, skateboard, or even yoga, you learn the rules, learn the process, then practice and practice that process.

Yes… Truly creative people do have a natural talent for their music, art, or sport. They seemed to be "gifted" and sometimes it comes naturally; however, we ALL can learn the skills necessary to be creative and innovative.

Being successful in any craft requires effort, and practice. You have to be committed to practice until your brain just does it automatically.

Here are some insightful quotes to will help you understand the process of becoming exceptionally innovative. They will be in Italics and at the end of each thought.

Many are from famous people, some are from unknown sources, some are funny, a lot of them will cause an "ah ha: moment for you, and others will make you stop and think for a moment. So, stop and think about these two quotes.

A man in New York asks a cab driver "How do you get to Carnegie Hall?" The cabbie answers "Practice, man, practice!"

In the 2008 book by Malcolm Gladwell, "10,000 Hour Rule" made famous by the movie Outliers: The Story of Success, 10,000 is the number of hours of practice needed to acquire mastery of a skill.

Definition Of Success

The son of the CEO of IBM, Thomas Watson Jr., pestered his dad Thomas Watson Senior, the Fonder of International Business Machines, IBM, to agree to give him $5m. He was to "go build his 'personal computer', which Tom Sr. thought was a fool's errand. The deal between them was when he ran out of money, Tom Jr. would never bring it up at a Board Meeting again.

Tom Sr. knew at IBM $5m wouldn't last long and his son's idea of creating a "P.C. then competing with the two kids from Cupertino would quickly fade.

Let me take a moment to say that the IBM P.C. or "Personal Computer" name was taken from a speech that Steve Jobs made calling the Apple II the world's first "Personal Computer". IBM made "mainframe" computers. The two kids from Cupertino made the world's first personal computer, but IBM took the term P.C. and ran with it.

Tom Jr. didn't have time to "design" a P.C. from the ground up the way the Steve's did. He had neither the time or the money. So he went to the same floppy drive company that was manufacturing the 5 1/4" floppies for Apple. They then made the drives for his machine. He took an obsolete chip IBM had laying around, the 8080 and threw together a motherboard. And, my favorite part of the story…

Did you ever ask yourself why the P.C. was always stuffed into a crappy metal box? It's because Tom Jr. didn't have the money or time to design a better enclosure. The story goes, he contracted with a heating ventilation & air conditioning (HVAC), ductwork metal shop to stamp out the enclosures from metals heating ducts.

Now all he needed was an operating system. When he asked the programmers at IBM to build one, they laughed at him. They all told him it would take years and millions of dollars to design one. So, Tom Jr. needed to buy one.

After searching the country for possible OS', the folks at IBM narrowed it down to two. One was a 2k Disk Operating System or DOS from Seattle and the second was a far superior operating system called CPM.

IBM selected the "kid's" OS from Seattle which became Microsoft.

The same happened to Elisha Grey. Do you know who he is? I didn't think so.

Alexander Bell registered his patent of the invention of the phone on February 14, 1876, Patent Number 174.465, which was confirmed by US Trademark and Patent Bureau in Washington, D.C. on March 7, 1876.

Only a few hours after Bell filed his patent, Elisha Grey, another inventor
registered his similar patent. Alexander Bell was granted the rights to the invention and the ownership of what would become one of the world´s most valuable patens.

See again, preparation and opportunity. Luck lightning struck Bell, but not Grey.

Don't let this discourage you! It happens to me and other companies and inventors all the time. It just means you have to keep trying. You need to keep being prepared. If you are prepared and an opportunity arises, you have a shot at success. And if Luck Lightning strikes you… Well… You made it!

"Aren't you glad that water is liquid at room temperature?"
-Lon Safko

Petroglyph Canyon - Perspective

When my youngest daughter was only eight, I took her on a hike in the Arizona desert to a place called Petroglyph Canyon. It was in the notorious Superstition Mountains which had a running waterfall nearly all year long. That is saying a great deal considering it wouldn't rain for months at a time and temperature often reached over 120 degrees F.

The hike was about 90 minutes each way with only a moderate climb up to the canyon. I knew it would be more than doable for an eight-year-old. And as always if you ever raise a child, about a half hour into the hike came the infamous "Daddy, are we there yet?" I calmly answered her, "No, sweetheart, not yet. Almost!"

Then, right on queue about 10 minutes later, "Daddy, are we there yet?" I calmly answered her again, "No, sweetheart, not yet. Almost!" This went on every 10 minutes for the next hour.

When we were about 20 minutes away, again she asked the question again. This time, I could see the actual canyon and a very large stone at the canyon's entrance. I looked down at her and said "See the canyon now? We are almost there!" She timidly replied, "I don't see the canyon, daddy."

Feeling a little frustrated I said "See the mountain on the left?", she answered, "Yes I do." I asked, "See the mountain on the right?" She answered "yes…" I further asked "Do you see where they come together, there is a very large boulder there? That's where we are going!" She answered, "No, I don't see the boulder."

Now, feeling even more frustrated, I asked again, "Do you see the mountain on the left?", she answered again "Yes daddy." I asked again "Do you see the mountain on the right?" She answered "yes…", again. I frustratedly asked, "Do you see where they come together, there is a very large boulder there, as big as a school bus on end?" She answered, "No, I don't see the boulder as big as a bus."

Now really frustrated and a little short, I got down on one knee and sternly asked "Do… You… See…" And, as I pointed to the canyon and looked up to see the boulder myself, I realized that she couldn't see it! It was impossible for her to see the boulder.

The trail rose up just enough that from her 4', eight-year-old perspective, the ground blocked her view. She couldn't see the canyon or the boulder no matter how many times I tried to explain it! From my 5' 10" perspective, I could see it without obstruction.

I had two immediate insights on that trial that day. One, sometimes no matter hard you look, there is something obstructing the view making it impossible to see the finish line. This made me think about how important it is for us to realize when and how we are being blocked every day by obstacles we aren't aware of. Obstacles placed in front of us by our parents, teachers, society, peers, bosses, clergy, and more. We have to be aware of these obstacles, know where and what they are, so you can be able to move past them to your final goal.

The second insight I had was no matter how much you try to teach a child, show examples to a child, or lecture a child, until they are ready to understand you and have the experience enough to put your lessons into perspective, they cannot understand the life lessons you are trying to teach them.

From that day on, I was significantly more patient with my daughter through her trials and tribulations even though I was sad I couldn't help her to prevent them.

"Five qualifications for success; training, experience, talent, passion, and luck."
-Lon Safko

CHAPTER 2

ORGANIC INNOVATION

Chapter 2

What Is Organic Innovation?

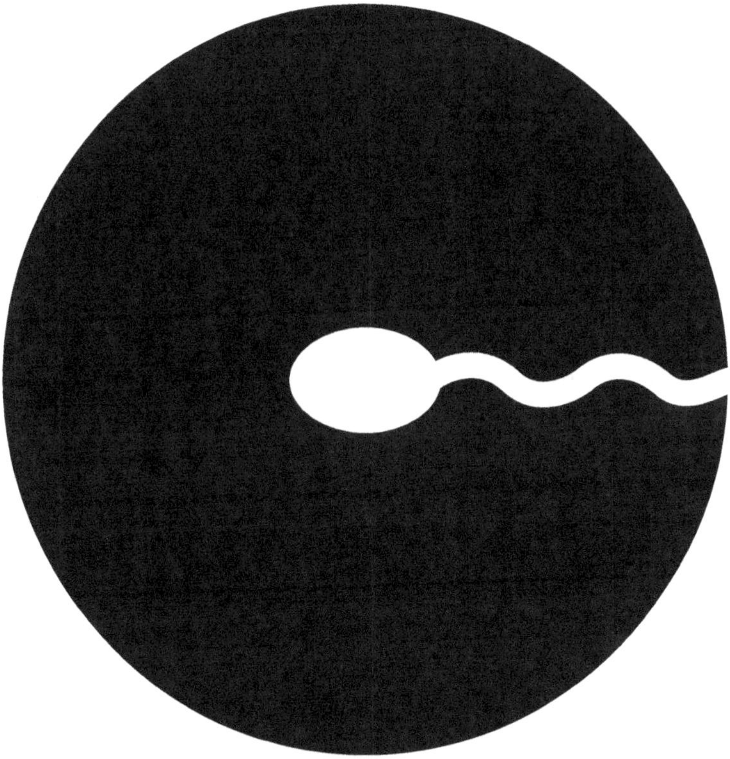

In this chapter, I wanted to discuss a new idea, a new way of looking at innovation. In the next chapter on Failure, I discuss when I lost my first company it was like losing a child.

This concept is critical for you to understand as it describes the life cycle of an idea and the emotion attachment we all have for our own creations. As you go through the rest of this book, keep this concept in mind and how it applies to all innovation.

Over the past several decades I have analyzed these feelings trying to make some sense of it all. The nurturing of an innovative idea was felt very organic. It felt personal. It was then that I realized, it was. Whether you give birth to a new life form or give birth to a new idea, they both required attention, nurturing, care, feeding, love, work, and growth.

In this chapter, we will look at innovation as if it were a living organism. From the very moment of its conception, inspiration, innovation, thought, idea, and invention each takes on a life of their own. This concept is out there, radical, and unusual, but if you want to think with a higher level of innovation, you need to change the way you think.

To that end, I wanted to share this idea, concept, or new life form with you in the hopes that you will become infected by it and help it spread, reproduce, and flourish.

The moment of innovation can be viewed as the conception or the beneficial mutation of an existing cell of an idea. There is a moment when an innovative idea exists when just a moment before it didn't.

Often an innovative idea is incomplete, only a zygote of a mature thought. This innovative thought must be nurtured, fed, and cared for until it is mature and has the ability to survive on its own.

While in this gestative stage the idea is difficult for others to comprehend. Its incompleteness prevents others from understanding its application and ultimate potential or what it could be when it grows up.

From the moment of inspiration or conception, the organic innovation's parent must grow this thought by feeding it with the nutrients of fresh perspectives, new information, and combine it with other mature and immature organic innovations until it develops into a mature thought or concept.

Once mature the organic innovation can venture out into the world on its own. It will be received by other people's perceptions and experiences. It will be held and cared for by others, some with the maternal instincts of its parent, others with only in passing curiosity, and some who wish to own or harm it.

An authentic innovative thought at this stage will become viral in nature. It will spread on its own accord without the help or encouragement of its parent. Once someone is exposed or comes in contact with this thought through their eyes and ears, their brain becomes infected with that thought. This idea will inhabit them and they will pass it on at will to others who are receptive to these ideas.

The more minor or underdeveloped the innovation, the less likely its survivability or replicability the organism will have. The more viable and mature the innovation is, the more likely this organism will be passed on from one human host to another.

This idea will incubate, be realized, and once again be passed on to another host where the process is repeated again and again. With modern telecommunications, email, blogs, websites, social media, text, YouTube, Snapchat, Instagram, Pinterest, and so many more digital media platforms, allows an organic innovation to be more infectious and spread faster than ever before. Word of mouth at the speed of light. A healthy viable thought will take on a life of its own and spread almost immediately, worldwide.

Sometimes lesser innovations will simply run their course and meet with their own genetic dead end. The innovation might fall out of favor, never be fully realized, become obsolete, or be surpassed by its own prodigy.

Occasionally, an innovation comes in contact with another similar, but slightly different thought and it will procreate. This procreation produces a prodigy where many of its inferior or recessive genes of the original idea are lost or ignored. The dominant genes of both parent ideas are combined to produce a thought or idea with a much higher pedigree. This process continually improves its ability to replicate, reproduce, spread, and recombine to grow into an even greater genetically enhanced organic innovation.

Often this organic innovation is accepted, put into practice, and becomes a permanent part of our culture. Once an innovation is widely accepted and put into practice, the idea becomes a building block for future innovative offspring that is often recombined to carry on the genes of its predecessor through generation after generation. These replications and future generations all contribute new positive mutations, spawning still other more infectious organic innovations.

Just as in life, these organic innovations continue to spread, mutate into even better and more complex organisms. Often, the more powerful ideas will jump species and recombine to propagate in a completely different industry or application. The most successful organic innovations will plant its DNA across many spectrums of different applications and will influence and change our lives as we know it for us and our descendants.

So, if you think this article about "organic innovation" has any merit at all, help it thrive, multiply, infect, propagate, recombine, and evolve into something new and never before seen by sharing it!

That's Organic Innovation!

It sometimes helps me to look at an innovative project in this light to get a better feel for my emotional attachment to the idea.

Here is a homework assignment: Take a few uninterrupted minutes to think about a project you have or are working on in the framework of "organic innovation" to see if any of these thoughts or feelings ring true for you. If it does, think about how you might look at that project and the way you interface with it, differently.

Steven Wright • Heads & Arms*

http://bit.ly/2BjYCQX

**Hello Steven,*
If you are reading this book and see my use of your joke sound bytes it's because I think you're the most innovative comedian I know and I want to drive people to your shows and recordings. We met at The Innovative Thinking Conference (IT) in Scottsdale, AZ in 1996. You kept calling me "Lon Chaney."

What Do You Do With An Idea?

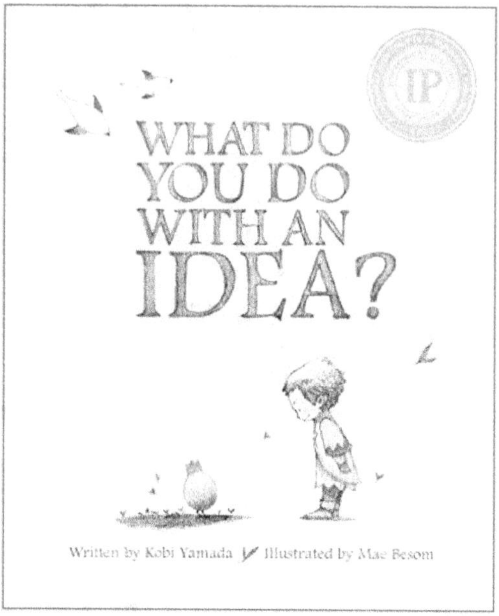

This is a great children's book on creativity another way to look at an idea as "organic innovation".

The book is called "What Do You Do With An Idea?" by Kobi Yamada. It's only about 20, one-paragraph pages and takes about 5 minutes to read, but it has the best description of how uncomfortable we are when we are challenged with a new idea. I wish I could put the story here for you, but as you know, because of copyrights, I can't. I will share a teaser of the first couple pages and encourage you to buy the book.

It's great for adults and children alike. Here is a sample of Kobi's book.

"One day I had an idea. Where did it come from" Why is it here? I wondered, "What do you do with an idea?" At first, I didn't think much about it. It seemed kind of strange and fragile. I didn't know what to do with it. So I just walked away from it. I acted like it didn't belong to me. But it followed me.

I worried what others would think. What would people say about my idea? I kept it to myself. I hid it away and didn't talk about it. I tried to act like everything was the same as it was before my idea showed up."… Homework: Get the book.

Henry Ford And His Assembly Line

We all know the story of Henry Ford and how he got credit for inventing the Assembly Line, and how it revolutionized manufacturing forever. But few know the story.

As this book isn't about Henry Ford, only innovation, I am forced to keep it brief.

Henry Ford did not invent the assembly line. That concept was routinely used in other industries; however, in the earliest part of the 20th century, companies and people like Louis Chevrolet, Ransom E. Olds (Oldsmobile), and Karl Benz, didn't use an assembly line either. Each car of the day was built by hand. Usually a car was built by 30 engineers working on one car for 30 days.

This intensive labor and long manufacture time made automobiles exceedingly expensive and only the very wealthy could afford one. Ford wanted to build a car for the common man. If he was to do

this, he needed to completely change the way his industry manufactured automobiles.

One day, Ford took his lunch pail and went to a nearby potato farm and sat under a tree. While eating his lunch he thought hard about how he could produce more cars faster than anyone else and thus make them cheaper.

He sat taking in nature while watching a farmer loading potatoes up a conveyor belt into a wagon. He was collecting vital information in a quiet non-interruptive environment. As he sat there thinking, he watched the potatoes moving he suddenly realized if he could swap out the potato for a car and had them moving down the conveyor belt to the engineers, rather than all the engineers working on one car at a time, the process would go exponentially faster. Also, if each engineer had only one job to do, he wouldn't need engineers. He could use unskilled labor.

By using the conveyor belt, speeding up the assembly, and reducing the labor costs, he could achieve his goal of manufacturing a low cost automobile everyone could afford.

Ford's use of the assembly-line allowed him to reduce the price of his touring car which cost in 1908 of $850 to less than $300 in 1925. Soon Ford's Model T comprised 40 percent of all cars sold in America. I also loved one of Ford's slogan about his Model T, "The customer can have it in any color they wish as long as it's black!"

The moral of the story is, don't look for solutions in your industry. If your industry had a solution to your problem, you would have already known about it. Open your mind to new ideas and look outside of your industry. Be receptive to everything around you!

As a side note, do you know why Ford's Model T was called the Model T? Because models A through S weren't very good! Even Ford failed that many times.

Henry Ford's Assembly Line Family Tree

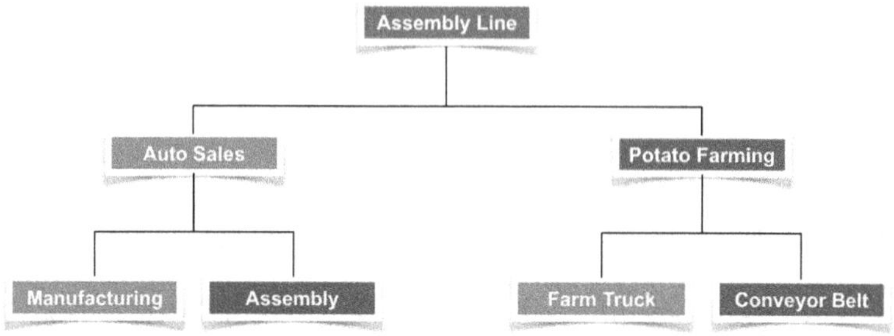

Family Tree

Looking at Ford's use of the assembly line with an "organic" perspective shows us it's family tree. Ford's need to solve his manufacturing problem of assembly was already solved in potato farming. It took an open mind, an uninterrupted environment, and "luck Lightning" to strike Henry that day under the tree for his right brain to see the solution, put the right pieces together in the right image, and communicate innovation to Henry's conscious mind for implementation.

Another important point here is nearly nothing is ever actually invented. Nothing "new" ever spontaneously combusts from nothing. While the iPhone is an amazing innovation, it just the concept of the telephone cell phone, camera / digital, computer that runs apps, and solid state circuitry / transistors, all in one very small, portable device.

See nothing new. The iPhone was just assembled out of previous innovations in a very unique, very small package. And if you look at the "smart phone", you can trace the telephony functions back to the flip phone, back to the "brick", back to the car phone, back to the touch tone landline home phone, back to the rotary phone, back to the party line, back to the flash call.

And, if you wanted to trace the smart phone's heritage and genetics further back, you could take it through Morse Code and back to the invention of electricity. Phew! That's organic Innovation. What can you see for the new, next generation?

Steven Wright • Subliminal Advertiser

http://bit.ly/2Cl0yDh

Look Elsewhere

The first collapsible baby carriage was invented by an inventor named Owen Maclaren. Maclaren was inspired by the system designed for folding undercarriages for Spitfire planes in World War II.

Innovator James Dyson was inspired by a cyclone vacuum system used to suck up sawdust in sawmills. Dyson went on to design the famous home vacuum.

Both innovators revolutionized previously well known designs from different industries. Let this be an additional reminder, if you are looking for a new way of doing something, look at different industries.

When asked where her creativity came from, Al Jean, one of the original writers for The Simpsons, said, "You get ideas from real life. Teachers you had, problems your kids are going through, things that happened to you as a kid, things you read in the paper."

The Simpsons are the longest continuously running sitcom in history topping out at nearly 30 years.

"Nothing is particularly hard if you divide it into small jobs."
-Henry Ford

The 30 Circles Test

- ✦ Take a piece of paper and draw 30 circles on it.

- ✦ You have one minute to turn as many circles as you can into objects.

Examples: One circle could be drawn as a sun. Another could be drawn as a globe.

Draw as many as you can! Look for quantity over quality.

Tip: Don't self-edit or be self-critical.

Remember, "Good artists copy, great artists steal."

How many were you able to convert? More than you thought? Less?

HOMEWORK ASSIGNMENT: Bookmark this page. Once you have finished reading this book, I want you to go back and try this test again. Compare the number of conversions today with the number of conversions then. I bet you will be surprised!

This creative exercise comes from researcher Bob McKim.

T. S. Eliot once wrote, "The immature poet imitates and the mature poet plagiarizes."

CHAPTER 3

FAILURE

Chapter 3

Failure On An Epic Scale

Let's kick off another first by talking about "failure" right out of the gate and get it out of the way.

It wouldn't be fair for me to just tout my successes and the successes of all the other people's examples. Yes, Henry Ford utilized the assembly line and the first mass-produced automobile. That's what we remember him for and what his biographies are written about. No one talks about his list of monumental failures or about how many times he was on the edge of bankruptcy. We never hear about all that.

We read that Thomas Edison was an amazing inventor with more patents that anyone in history with 1093 U.S. Patents, but we seldom read about all his failures, about the "10,000 ways NOT to make a lightbulb".

As the author of this book on "innovation", I have a responsibility to you, to present both sides of success and failure. Please, don't think for a moment that every one of my "innovations" was successful. It was the continuous ups and downs that earned me the right to write, teach and speak, about innovation. It's much more from my failures that have earned the badge of courage and by far the better lessons.

For every success, I have had three or more failures. And, I didn't just fail. We are talking about failure of epic proportions. Mushroom cloud failures. However, this is where I learned my most valuable lessons. It was these mistakes that I most likely will never make again.

Being successful doesn't teach you anything. When you succeed, you say to yourself "Of course that worked. I knew it!". It's when you fail you ask W.T.F.? (Why The Face?) How did that happen? What could I have done to avoid that? Why didn't I see that coming? How can I do it better next time? If I did it better now, would this idea be a success? Should I keep trying to "give up the ghost?"

By the way, the last question is always the toughest to answer. An entrepreneur knowing when to give up on their brain-child and walk away is nearly impossible to be impartial. You have to listen to others and trust those closest to you.

Here's a couple of examples of ideas that should have worked, but didn't.

2001, Digit Rights Distribution

Here's a great idea I had in 2001. Remember, the Internet was only 6 years old in 2001. We were about to hit head-on into the "Dot-Bomb" era where the entire Internet economy collapsed because banner ads and "impressions" didn't translate the same way they were used in media. We were told a banner ad impression was just as valuable as a TV viewer's or a radio listener's, or a newspaper reader's impression was. Today it's true, none of them have next to no value at all.

This was the year I decided to speak and train full time. I needed a website (which I already had since 1996, a one-sheet, which I could put up on my website, and a "sizzle-reel", a demo video. So like most other speakers, I had a demo tape filmed and multiple copies made to send out to prospective clients and speakers bureaus.

Since I had been making my own CDs since 1996. It's hard to imagine that a technology now obsolete was so new and cutting edge at one. The blank CD's cost me $2.50 each in 2001 dollars. But I knew that "digital" was the wave of the future. As a result, I made dozens of CD duplicates. Later, I found out that no one had CD players for the P.C.'s yet. That was also in the future.

Realizing if the video tapes were digitized, the videos could be distributed, downloaded, and even viewed online. I know… I know. Considering that YouTube has 1,300,000,000 users, there are 300 hours of video are uploaded to YouTube every minute, almost 5 billion videos are watched on Youtube every single day, and YouTube gets over 30 million visitors per day it's hard to believe everyone didn't see that coming… But they didn't!

That's when I created "Digital Media Distribution". Knowing if I could get 100's of professional speakers to pay me a fee to transfer their 1/2" VHS video tapes to digital I could make a killing! I also developed the idea that… Wait for it… I could create a website that housed all those speaker's videos for which I would charge a monthly fee, and prospects and bureaus could go to the site and watch the videos in the convenience of their own P.C.'s, I would make a double killing!

Well, it didn't work. After trying to get speakers to sign up for the translation service, they couldn't understand the need for "digital". The "norm" was VHS Tapes. Every office had a VHS tape player. Absolutely no one was interested in the service. OMG?!

The next most valuable feedback was "Speakers will put their videos on a website that offered other speakers!" "There is no way I am going to send one of my prospects to a website where they could see other speakers (possibly a better speaker than me), and take a chance they would hire them instead of me! No way!"

Crash and burn.

2006, V-Centives

In 2006, I had another idea where I could pay people in gift cards. Think about it for a moment from all the angles.

The first fact you must become aware of is Cost of Customer Acquisition. That is the actual cost a company spends to acquire just one customer, either a new customer or to replace an existing customer.

While these numbers are VERY difficult to find, here are some numbers on Industry Cost of Customer Acquisition. They are amazing:

Travel		**Telecom**	
Priceline.com:	$7	Sprint PCS:	$315
		Nextel:	$430
Retail			
Index of 74 Retailiers:	$14	**Financial**	
Barnesandnoble.com:	$10	TD Waterhouse:	$175
Amazon:	$29	Ameritrade:	$202
Direct Catalogs:	$15	E-Trade:	$272
		Credit Cards:	$150
Magazines		Mortgages:	$300–$700
Consumer Magazines:	$48		
		Automobiles:	
Satellite/Cable			
XM Satellite Radio:	$123	**RV's:**	$900
Cable Companies:	$150		
Direct Satellite:	$400	**New Homes:**	$2,100
DirectTV:	$550		

If a retailer has to spend say, $14 in advertising to acquire only one customer, then give me a fist full of $10 gift cards and I will give them to people who want to buy your products. They will buy your products, they will experience your great customer experience, they will begin their buying relationship with a gift card (which is fun), and you will save $4 from your usual cost. AND… if you read my blog "Are Gift Cards A Scam", the facts show that 40% of all gift cards given are lost or never redeemed. That is a ton of revenue for all retailers!

If 100's of companies gave me thousands of gift cards, my part to satisfy the retailer would be to distribute them and I could either use them as currency or sell them for pennies on the dollar (anyone ever heard of Groupon?).

Nope… A total crash and burn.

To this day I am dumbfounded that this didn't take off. It's funny how some things at a given point in time doesn't look like a good idea, but several years later, it's commonplace. Amazon is a perfect example.

When Jeff Bezos founded Amazon on July 5, 1994, NO ONE would buy anything online. Not then and not for more than a decade later. Jeff burned through millions of venture capital dollars. He tried to convince the world that buying stuff online then having it brought to your home was a good idea. The common mindset of people wasn't to buy anything unless they could see it, touch it, and feel it. Well that all changed.

The problem was, Jeff had to wait (and fund) more than 10 years worth of societal change before the thinking for the world around him could catch up to his innovation.

The moral of the story is… Hang in there! If it was easy, everybody would do it! You can too!

"Discover the fourth primary color!"
-Lon Safko

The Failure Continues

Here are two more quick examples of failure from companies and products you are familiar with.

WD40

How about WD40. It stands for Water Displacement, 40th Formulation attempt. It was invented during World War II when the military was looking for a way to keep wires and other parts dry and water-free, but not use a petroleum product that would corrode or eat through the wires.

Did you know that WD40 is made with fish oil and is edible?

Angry Birds

How about Angry Birds? did you know how much that that little app was worth?

Rovio's company valuation in 2012 was around $210 million, but its real valuation is probably better assessed from a rejected buyout offer from Zynga for $2.25 billion. Their IPO valuation is set at $2 billion dollars. Their animated film based on Rovio's Angry Birds has earned around $150 million in global ticket sales alone.

Angry Birds was the 52nd game Rovio created. See... Preparation, Opportunity, but you need the Luck Lightning?

Line Extensions That Failed

It seems like every major company (and individuals) have had their share of failures.
Let's take a look at a few more epic failures by the brands we know and love.

- **Fruit of the Loom laundry detergent**
  We'll make them, you stain them, we'll clean them (my slogan not their's.)

- **Kleenex Baby Diapers**
  We'll wipe both ends. (Not their slogan, again.)

- **Heinz Cleaning Vinegar**
  We can clean up anything you ate. (mine.)

- **Vaseline Suntan Lotion**
  When you thinking sun and sand, your thinking being covered in Vaseline (yep, not theirs.)

- **Gillette Antiperspirant**
  We'll keep them hairless and smelling fresh. (Armpits…)

- **Harley-Davidson Wine Coolers**
  (I don't even know where to begin with this one… Harley-Wine-Coolers? really!)

These are all real brand extensions. You can't make this stuff up.

"Aren't you glad, that you have opposing thumbs?"
-Lon Safko

Sometimes when an idea fails, it's just a bad idea. Not all ideas are good ideas. It's up to us to be able to distingue the difference and not invest any more time or money into ideas that will never work. Good luck knowing the difference.

Then friggin' "Pet Rocks" come along and throws all that out the window. Sometimes there's just no telling what will be a success.

(In 1975, advertising executive Gary Dahl invented the Pet Rock and Dahl sold 1.5 million Pet Rocks for $3.95 each, with discounts earned him $15 million dollars)

"Why is the word 'short' longer than the word 'long'?"
-Lon Safko

Failure Times Five

The most important part of failure is not to take it personally. Later on in this book, I will discuss a new concept of "Organic Innovation". This is where you look at your idea or creation as that, a creation. Many entrepreneurs see their creations as a child.

You give birth to the idea, you nurture it, grow it, sacrifice for it, sometimes for years. If you are lucky, you can watch it get out into the world on its own and succeed! But, sometimes, you watch it die.

When I lost my first company, I was devastated. I spend so much energy building that idea only to watch someone come along and kill it. I felt helpless because there was nothing within my power I could do to prevent its death. It was out of my hands. All the money I could throw at it wouldn't change the outcome.

At the time, I didn't realize that I was reacting the way a father or parent would react. I didn't understand that I was actually grieving a loss, the loss of an idea I gave birth to.

Looking back, I completely realize I went through the five stages of grief. Really! One stage at a time, I dragged myself and my family through all five stages; denial, anger, bargaining, depression, and acceptance. And, during this time, I couldn't function. Looking for a "job" was extremely difficult. Being innovative was impossible!

At first, I couldn't believe it was over, it was dead, and it wasn't coming back. Then I really did get angry! Angry at everybody! The people who cause it. The people who might have been able to prevent it. Even people that had nothing to do with its demise. I even got angry with my family and spouse. Of course, at the time, I didn't know why I was so angry and I didn't know how to stop being angry.

Then came the bargaining. I bargained with shareholders, suppliers, and even employees. None of that changed the outcome. Then came depression. That wasn't pretty. It was tough to do most anything, especially being my usual upbeat entrepreneur. This part lasted for more than a year.

Then finally came acceptance! Yea for acceptance! At that point, I moved on and invented my next company that to date generated three U.S. Patents, 45,000 customers, and more than $1m in revenue.

So let me give you a very valuable word of advice here… Get over it! Don't take it personally! Crap happens! People can't be trusted! It's not about you! Move on!

Seriously, you cannot take it personally. If you could have controlled it, you would have. Let it go, say to yourself, "business is business" (and if you say it in a Yiddish accent it's even funnier), and free your mind of anything negative so you can find your next success.

And… If you can do that… Email me immediately on how.

Steven Wright • 24 Hour Banking

http://bit.ly/2jBpAPp

CHAPTER 4

YOUR BRAIN

Chapter 4

Your Brain

This Is Your Brain…

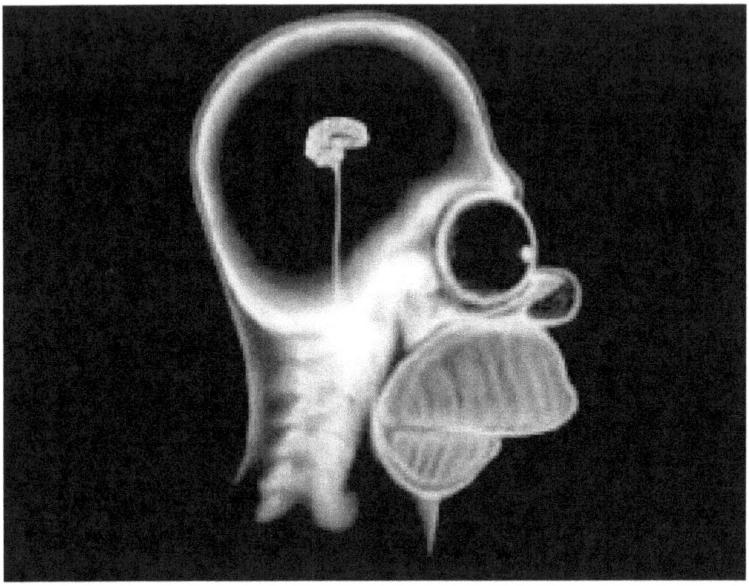

"Anticipation is worth more than surprise."
-Lon

This is your brain on Innovation!

"Don't ever work for an organization that lacks the insight to hire you."
-Lon Safko

Let's talk about the brain… Your brain. Scientists and psychologists discovered long ago, generally speaking, analytical thinking is done on the left side of your brain while creativity is done on the right side of your brain.

Of course this is a gross generalization and in fact, when challenged with a task, many areas of the brain light up in the fMRI, showing that it takes a lot of your brain to find a solution. Creativity takes image processing, long memory; both short term and long term memory, and many other areas. Generally speaking, creativity lights up the right and analytics light up your left sides. For the purpose of this book, that how we will refer to it.

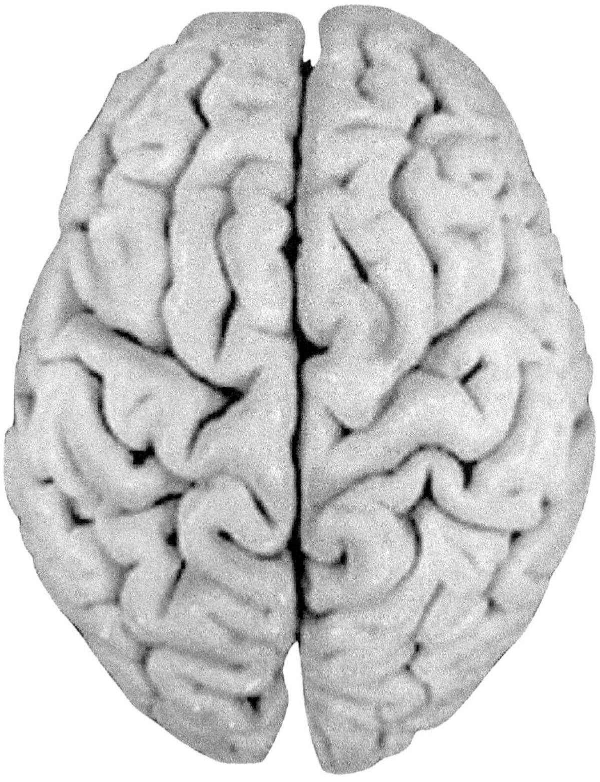

Your Left Brain
Analytical

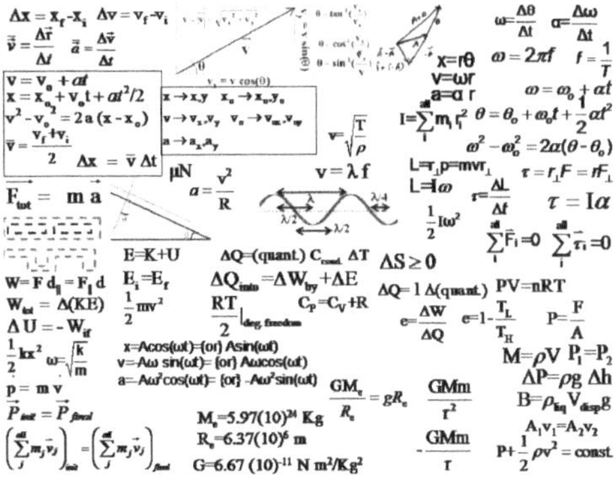

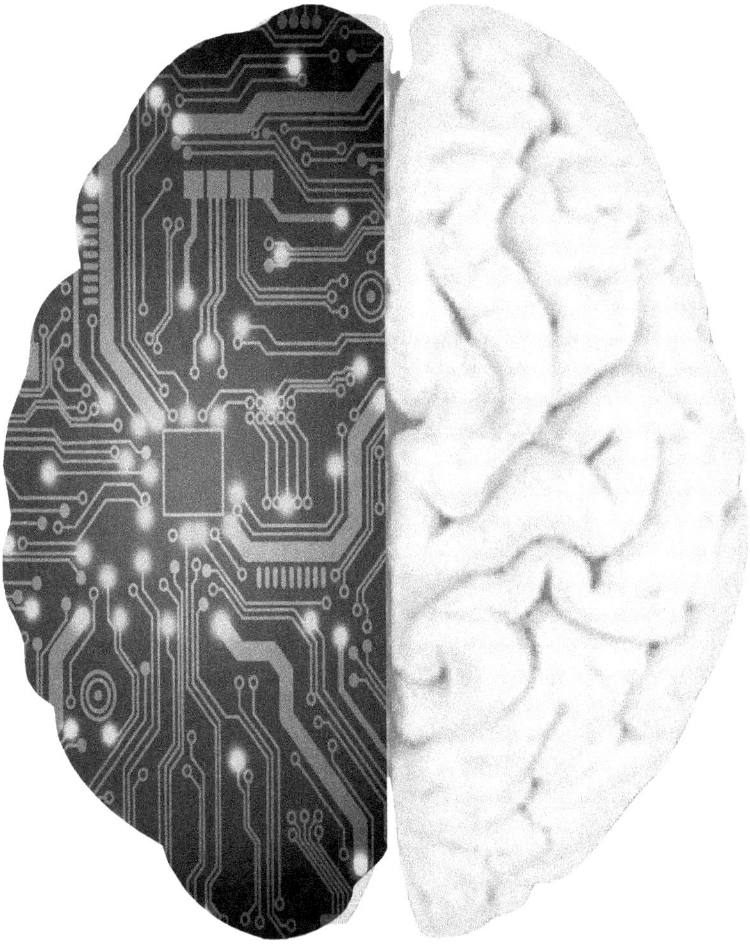

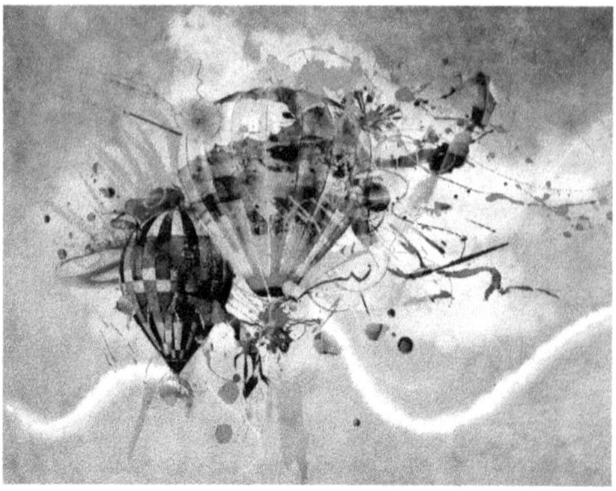

Your Right Brain
Creative

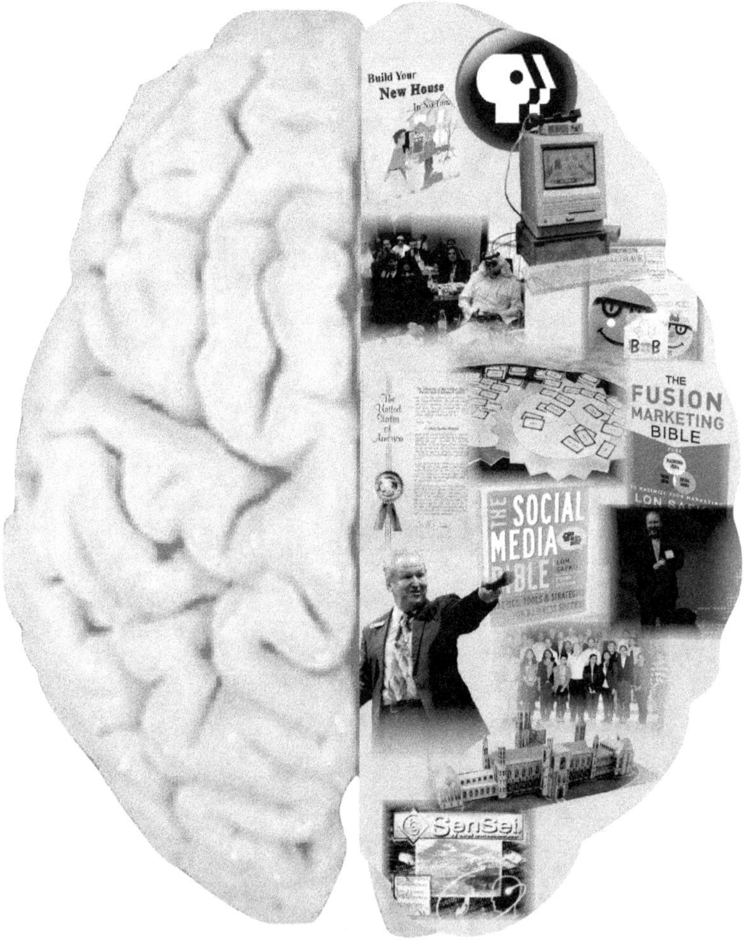

Characteristics of Left Brain Thinkers

Here are some words that generally describe the thinking patterns of a right brain thinker. Can you think of other Words?

Calculate, Analytical, Linear, Explicit, Sequential, Numbers, Concrete, Rational, Active, Goal-Oriented, Verbal, and Numbers

Take a moment to write down some words that describe your right brain thinking. *(Remember… You have to do the exercises!)*

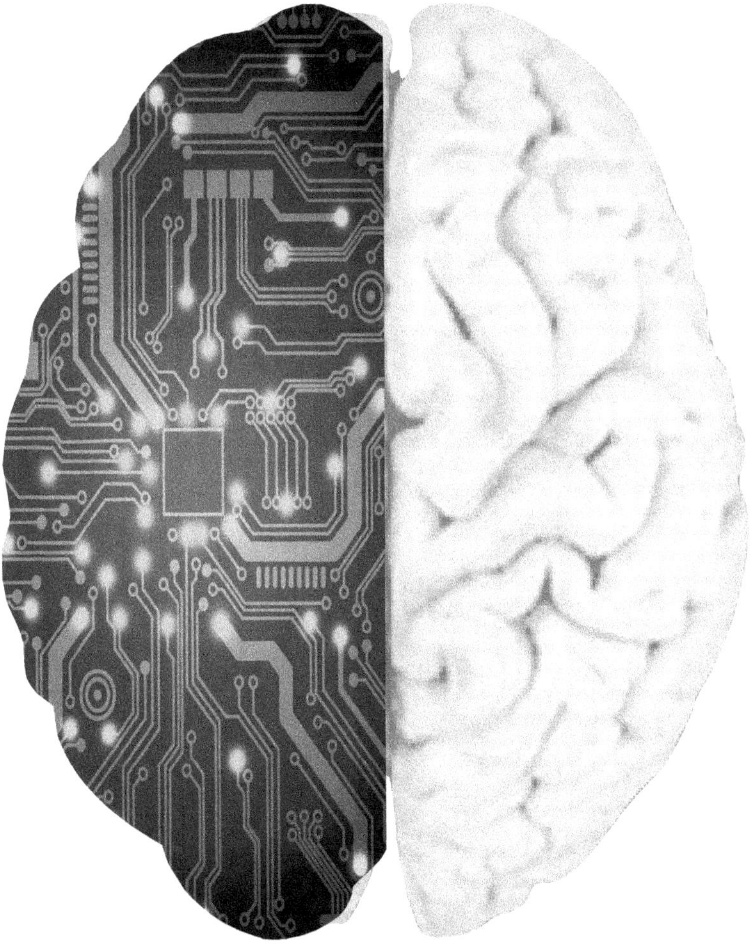

Characteristics of Right Brain Thinkers

Here are some words that generally describe the thinking patterns of a right brain thinker.

Can you think of other words?

Shapes, Colors, Concepts, Intuitive, Spontaneous, Emotional, Nonverbal, Holistic, Playful, Diffuse, Symbolic, and Physical

Take a moment to write down some words that describe your right brain thinking.

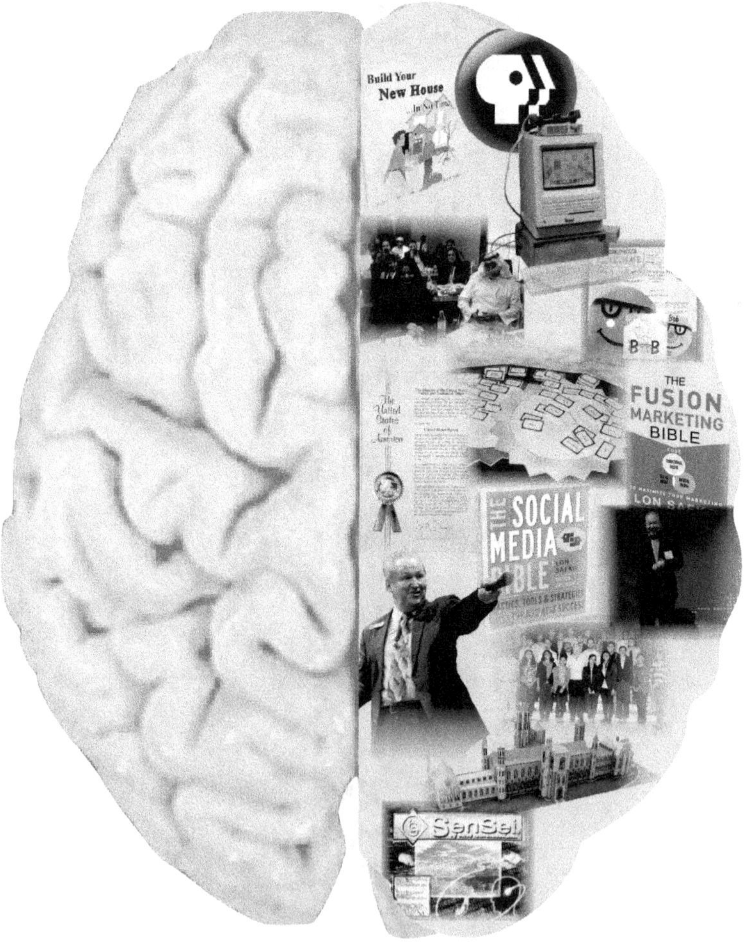

Analytical / Creative

It's impossible to do two things at once. No matter how cool you think you are. There is NO such thing as multitasking. What you can do is switch between tasks, not undertake two tasks at the same time. When you are switching between tasks, you are doing neither, well.

Come on, you know it's true. If you want to do a job well, concentration is key. Other task are simply distractions. If you want to be creative and really innovative, you need to believe this and create an environment without distraction. Set aside a certain amount of time, put your phone in a different room, step away from your computer, stay away from your email and especially YouTube, put on some background, non-distracting music and focus.

"Aren't you glad, that the sun rises in the same spot?"
-Lon Safko

Steven Wright • Straw Wrapper

http://bit.ly/2iuVDwS

Moldy Bread

When Alexander Fleming discovered penicillin in 1923, he was in a "creative" frame of mind that morning. If instead, he was in his usual "analytical" mindset, concentrating on his cultures in the dishes, he would have noticed the one dish without culture activity and simply thrown it away. To an analytical mind, an empty culture dish is of no relevance or use. His would have viewed it as an error when he had expected bacterial activity. In his creative mind, it was a clue to something bigger and he asked the question "why was there an absence of bacteria cultures acting in the dish?'

The rest is what they say, "history".

"You can't lose if you refuse to quit!"
-Lon Safko

A Doodle Story

"A" is for Activity!

1. Create a squiggle on a piece of paper.
2. Use a phrase from the list below (or create one of your own).
3. Transform your squiggle into a doodle, that visually expresses the phrase in some way. It could be literal or just a response to the phrase.

- ✦ Happy as a clam
- ✦ I can't get no satisfaction
- ✦ Where in the world?
- ✦ A hard day's night
- ✦ Human nature
- ✦ Is there a doctor in the house?
- ✦ The art of noise
- ✦ Here comes trouble
- ✦ Abracadabra!
- ✦ What's that sound?

Go on... Take a moment... Do it...

"The difference between knowledge and wisdom is experience."
-Lon Safko

Where Does Creativity Hide

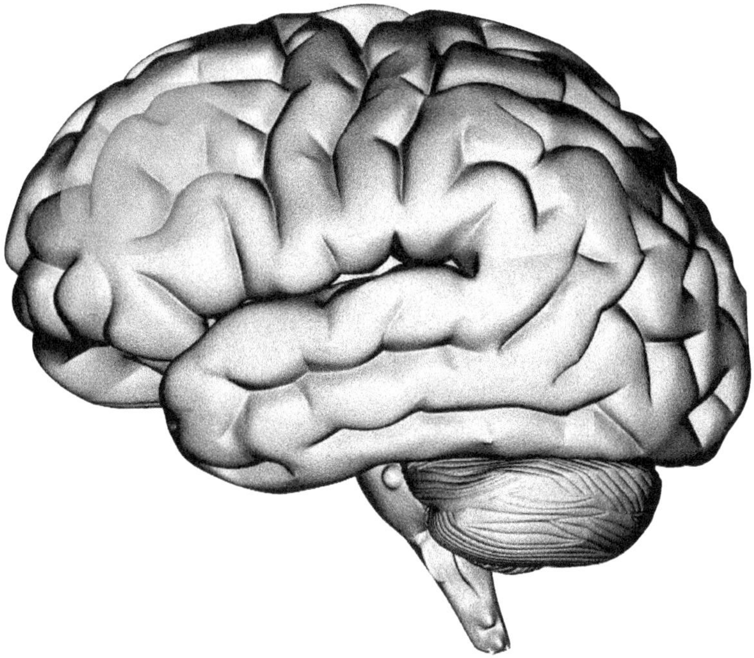

Dorsolateral Prefrontal Cortex

Getting technical, it's the Dorsolateral Prefrontal Cortex that controls a person's will to live, personality, and has been implicated in planning complex cognitive behavior, personality expression, decision making, and moderating social behavior. It is our filter or "gatekeeper". If a creative thought wants to surface and make itself known, you have to train your DPC to allow innovation through and not what you think about your mother-in-law or boss. This takes practice.

"Aren't you glad, that steel is solid at room temperature?"
-Lon Safko

How Many "F"s

Here's another exercise for your brain. Simply count the number of "F"s there are in this sentence?

FINISHED FILES ARE THE RESULT OF YEARS OF SCIENTIFIC STUDY COMBINED WITH THE EXPERIENCE OF YEARS...

"Aren't you glad, that your skin is waterproof?"
-Lon Safko

The correct answer is 6. There are 6 "F"s. It is very likely you got a different number, probably less than 6. It's difficult to count the number of "F"s that follow the letter "O" as in the word "OF".

When our brain processes the word "OF", it thinks "OV", not "OF", so it skips that "F" in the count. You can't even trust your own brain. It's like the old joke about a cheating husband who is caught by his wife in beds with his lover and he yells, "It's not what you think! Are you going to believe me or your own eyes!" If he was yelling about the number of "F"s, he'd be right!

A solution to solving this is to read it backward. Start at the end and slowly process the letter towards the beginning. This way it is less likely your brain will lock on the pattern of the word and decide whether or not it should be considered.

Here's a fun tip. Do you want to solve maze puzzles faster than anyone? Start at the end of the maze. The mazes were designed to be difficult to solve when you start where they tell you to. It was designed that way. If you start at the end, you will find in most cases, you can draw a single line right back to the starting position. Try it with the maze below. Just use your eyes to trace the route through the maze.

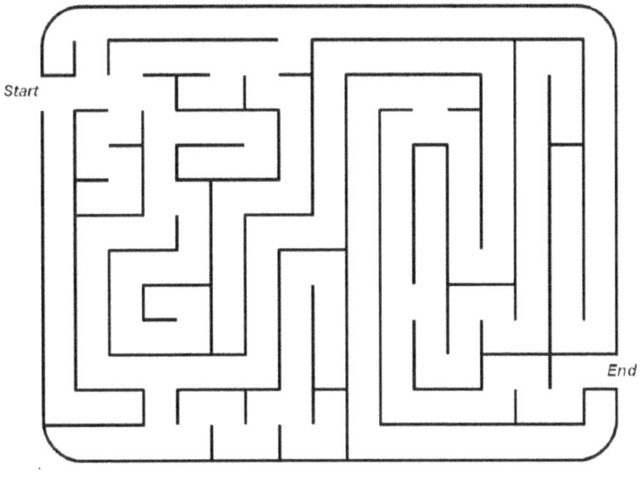

Try To Read This

Read this aloud…

I cdnuolt bivelee taht I cluod aulacity uesdnatnrd waht I was rdanieg. The phaonmneal pweor of the hmuan mnid. Aoccdrnig to rscheearch at Cmabrigde Uinervtisy, it deosn't mttaer ni waht
oredr the Itteers in a wrod are, the olny iprmoatnt tihng is taht the frist and Isat Itteer be in the rghit pclae. The rset can be a taotl mses and you can sitll raed it wouthit a porbelm. Tihs is bcuseae the huamn mnid deos not raed ervey Iteter by istlef, but the wrod as a wlohe. Amzanig huh?
Yaeh and I awlyas thought slpeling was ipmorantt!

Mind blown?

"No, just means you have to try it a different way."
-Lon

The reason you can read this so easily is because your eyes don't start with the first word, look at the character, move right until is sees a space, then determines that must be a word, then looks for "st", or "th", or "ou", or "tt", or other consonant pairs, then analyzes vowel pairs, then match it up to "when tow vowels go walking the first one does the talking", "a", "i", "o", "u", sometimes "y" and "w", except the second month alone to which we assign 29, gathers no moss… Yikes! It would take a week to read this last paragraph.

No, the brain does separate words by space, quickly, then looks at the first and last character only. It estimates the overall size of the word, matches that pattern with words it had read previously, then guesses what the word is. If it fits in context, then it knows it guessed correctly. If it doesn't fit, the brain pulls up the next best visual match.

"Inspiration is when two or more common concepts fit together to form a unique solution."
-Lon Safko

The Stroop Effect

In this challenge, you will need to create the chart below in your word processor. Type the two columns of words that you see below. Then, Change the text to the colors in the parentheses; e.g.: the YELLOW is printed in (Green), the BLACK is printed in (Yellow), etc.

YELLOW(Green)	BLACK(Yellow)
PURPLE(Red)	ORANGE(Black)
BLUE(Green)	GREEN(Blue)
BLUE(Red)	RED(Blue)
YELLOW(Blue)	GREEN(Red)
RED(Blue)	BLUE(Red)
ORANGE(Blue)	GREEN(Black)
RED(Green)	[illegible]
PURPLE(Black)	ORANGE(Orange)

Challenge #1: Start in the top right corner with the first word on the list. Quickly, say the word, not the color. Read all the words in both lists.

Go!

Challenge #2: Read the words again, only say the color of the word, not the word.

Go!

Did you see any difference in your ability to read the words versus telling the colors? I bet you did a lot better on the first challenge and found the second challenge difficult. Why would that be? It's very simple. Any pre-kindergarten kid knows their colors.

It's because you are experiencing the Stroop effect, named after psychologist John Ridley Stroop.

This test shows how dominant your left brain is. You analytical brain is what keeps you alive by constantly analyzing the world around you and trying to determine what's important to your safety and what can be ignored. Let's look at some of the data that is streaming into your brain right now that the left side of your brain is disposing of as nonessential.

Do you feel the chair pressing up against your butt? Do you hear the hum of the printer? The traffic outside? Your waistband? The armrests on your chair? Your shoes? The room temperature may be a little warn or a little too cool? Your hair? Can you feel your hair?

All this and thousands of more data inputs are streaming into your brain through every sensor your body has, but only information that your left brain thinks is important is getting in.

Your left brain presses the words, so reading the words in spite of their color and be done quite easily. The left / analytical brain reads the words and spits them out. Just like that.

The problem comes in when you are determining colors. Remember from above. The right side of your brain the creative side which processes colors. When you try the second challenge and read only the colors, your right brain has to determine the color then relay that information to the gatekeeper, you left brain to analytically yell it our (either out of your mouth or into your head-voice). This takes an extra step and your left brain needs to verify the information first as important enough to pass on.

Damn dominant brain! It's this crossover that slows our creativity and sometimes prohibits our ability to "realize" our innovation.

As with all problems, the first step is to admit you have a problem. The second step is to be aware of this and to practice overcoming our "condition". With practice, the crossover comes faster and with less effort.

"My ultimate goal is to find a cure for entropy."
-Lon Safko

Steven Wright • Different Sox

http://bit.ly/2ivA0fW

CHAPTER 5

INNOVATION & CREATIVITY

?>!

Chapter 5

Innovation vs Creativity

in·no·va·tion
/inə'vāSH(ə)n/
noun
1. the action or process of innovating.
2. synonyms: change, alteration, revolution, upheaval, transformation, metamorphosis,
breakthrough;
3. a new method, idea, product, etc.
plural noun: innovations "technological innovations designed to save energy"

cre·a·tiv·i·ty
/krēā'tivədē/
noun
1. the use of the imagination or original ideas, especially in the production of an artistic work.
2. synonyms: inventiveness, imagination, innovation, innovativeness, originality, individuality.

Mistakes Are Opportunities

Often, the truly creative solutions to a problem aren't where we expect to find it. We can look and look in a particular place for an answer, then suddenly, we'll find the answer somewhere else.

Serendipity: A moment of inspiration where you creatively find answers when you look at one thing then, but by a lucky accident, you see another.

Example: Constantine Fahlberg was working with a new combination of chemicals in 1879 and rubbed an itching lip without washing his hands. The sweet substance he tasted when he licked his lips became saccharin, a substitute for sugar.

"An Innovator is someone who can discern patterns where none exist"
-Lon Safko

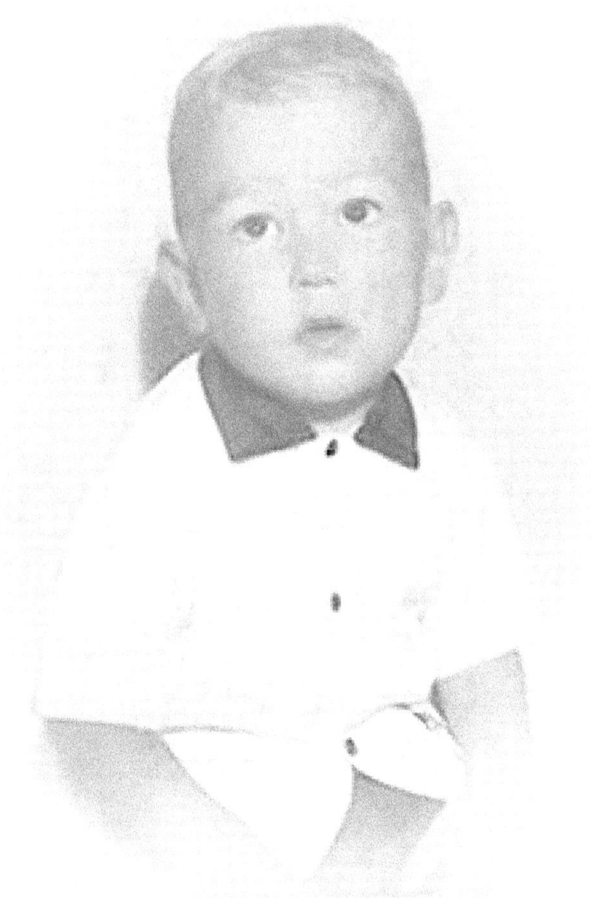

Celebrate Your Internal Child

Recently a group of 2nd graders was asked if they considered themselves "creative" 90% of the kids said yes, they felt they were creative. A group of high school students was asked if they felt they were creative and only 5% considered themselves creative. What happens to us? How do we all go from being creative to not?

"The difference between hearing and listening is comprehension."
-Lon Safko

Steven Wright • Batteries Not Included

http://bit.ly/2zRfPCU

Celebrate Your Internal Child

Let's go back to where you were as a child. Not the location, but where your head was at. What did you love to do as a child? What was your favorite pass time?

Tell me! Seriously, tell me!

Write down some activities you really enjoyed as a child. Try to remember how you felt when you did them. Who did you do it with? How did you feel when you were doing it.

Here's what happened to your creativity.

It was taken away by your parents, grandparents, teachers, pastors, priests, nuns, reverends, rabbis, and other 'authority" figures in your life. People you trusted.

Our guardians believed if we conformed and did what everyone was expected to do, we'd be more successful. Don't chew gum, stand in a straight line, no talking, follow the person in front of you, sit upright in your chair, and don't question authority. It was this last one that got me kicked out of Catholic School in the second week of the fourth grade. And, probably all the other too.

Our parents thought if we paid attention and did what everyone else did, we wouldn't get in trouble, teachers would like us, we would get a better education and graduate. They further believed if we "straighten up and fly right", we would fit in better and get a better job, get along with our bosses, make more money and overall have a happier life. All those rules about killed me!

I questioned everything and didn't accept "Because I told you so!", or "That's just the way it is!" I always wanted to know why and I still do! You need to as well. Never take anything for granted. Never go with the status quo. If you want to be more creative, you first have to give yourself permission to think differently than everyone else.

This might sound easy, but it difficult to accomplish. We, humans, are herd animals. We find safety and comfort in the herd. We are not comfortable standing out, be different, or be made fun of. But... If you want to stand out and be outstanding, then you have to make a conscious effort.

You have to allow yourself to be different, think different, act different, and this is difficult. If you practice this, you'll find eventually it becomes fun! My 6 grandkids call me Papa-Monkeyhead for a reason.

I got (and keep that title) because I am not like the other grandparents. I have fun with the kids. I challenge them and encourage them to break the rules, question everything, and do things their own way. And, when I get them in that frame of mind... I give them back to their parents.

These actions are two-fold. I allow the kids to get-out-of-box, think differently, be more creative. It also allows me to get even with my kids for being brats when they were younger. Oh yeah, be sure to add an ample amount of sugar to this mix.

"Innovation: Mixing common elements to form an uncommon solution."
-Lon Safko

Draw Yourself

Get another piece of paper and a pen. Now, draw a picture of yourself as you would if you were in the 1st grade again. Think about it before you start. Draw the picture of yourself and write your name next to it. Here's the catch…

USING YOUR LESS DOMINANT HAND!

Important note: If any of the images you draw of yourself look anything like these images, seek immediate professional attention! Dial 911!

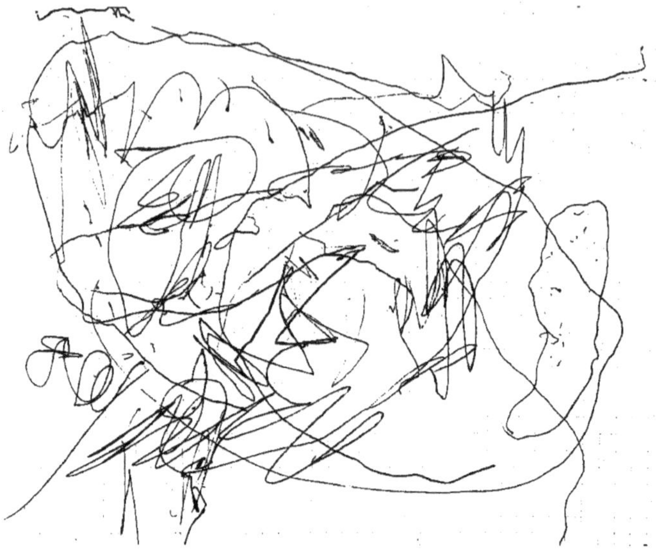

"Innovation: Cognitive Olympics"
-Lon Safko

The Torrance Test

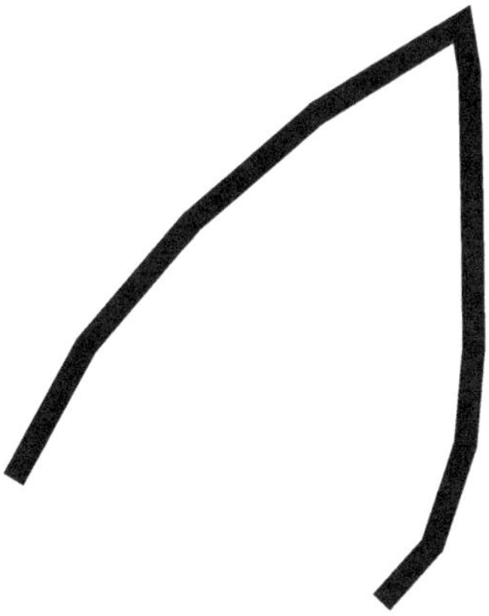

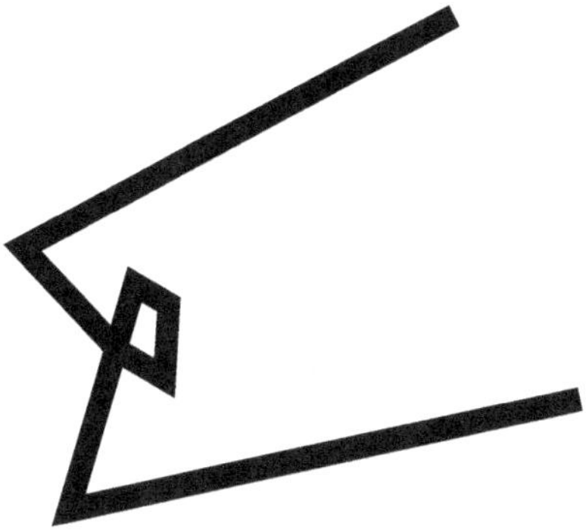

The Torrance Test was developed in the 1960s by psychologist Ellis Paul Torrance, he called it the Torrance Test of Creative Thinking. He used these two images to test his subjects:

Let's begin by drawing two large 3 x 3 grids similar to the one below only larger.

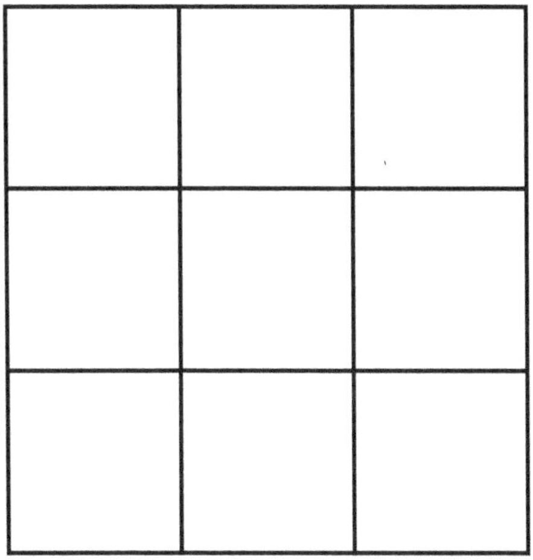

In the first 3 x 3 grid, start with the first box and draw the first Torrance image:

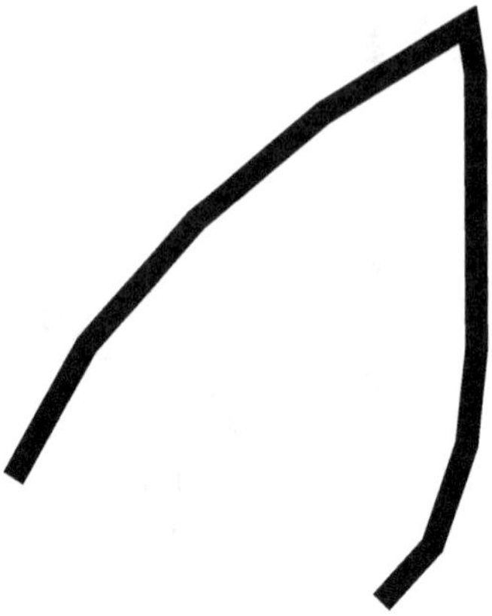

Then, complete the image by adding your own interpretation using those lines as a start. Here are a few images that others have drawn. Take your time before you put your pencil to the paper. In the right side of your brain, see where in an image does the Torrance image fit. Then simply complete that image. Repeat this process for all nine square.

Here's the catch… You have three minutes.

Go!

"Aren't you glad, that gravity is constant?"
-Lon Safko

Here are some examples of what others have done with those lines.

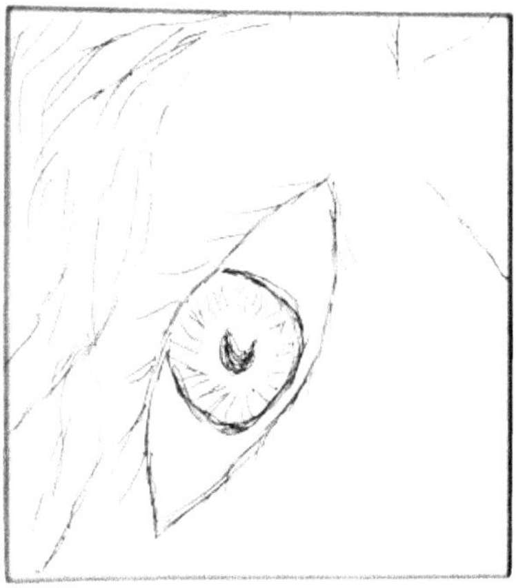

"Success equals a little vision, followed by a great deal of tenacity!"
-Lon Safko

In the second grid, repeat the exercise with this Torrance Image and see what your creative brain can come up with. Once again, use all nine squares and you have 3 minutes.

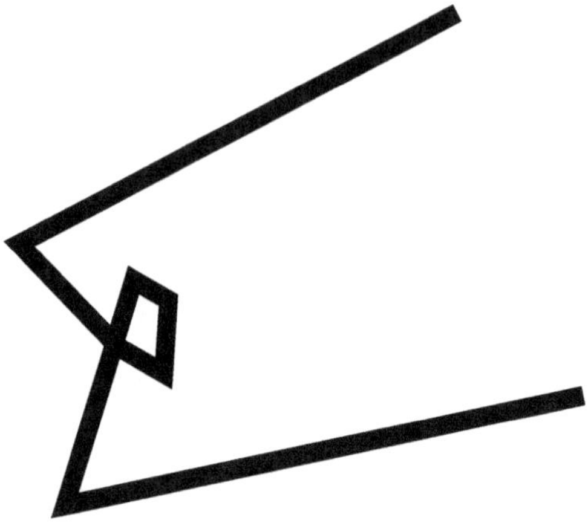

Go!

Come on! That why it's called an exercise!

Here are some examples of what others have seen in their mind's eye.

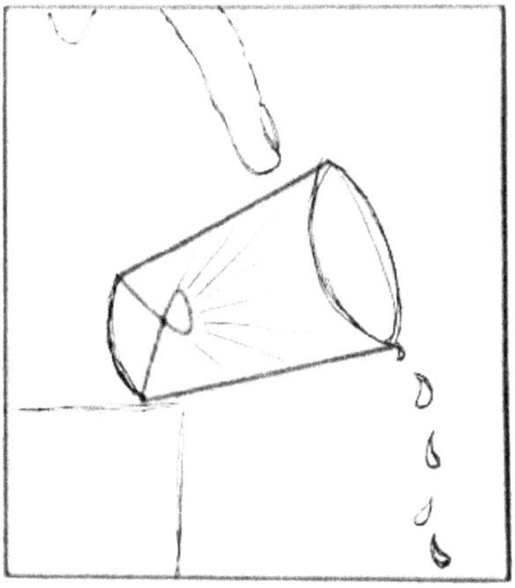

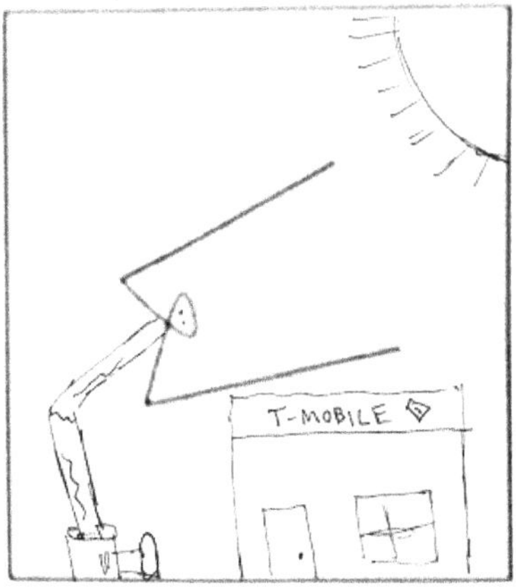

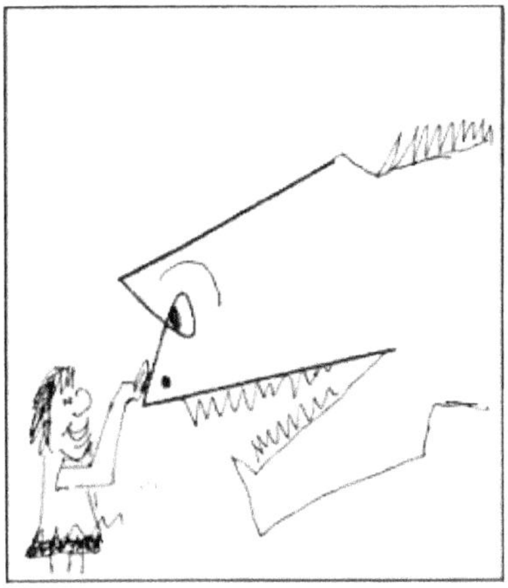

"Why does the moon sometimes come out in the day, but the sun never comes out at night."
-Lon Safko

Time To Be Creative

Bring In The Experts - Video

http://bit.ly/2iwLlfE

Creativity Calisthenics

The British Psychological Society's Research Digest Blog (how about that name…), reported on interesting research that shows that shifting your eyes horizontally back and forth for 30 seconds can boost creativity.

Apparently, it helps with communication between both

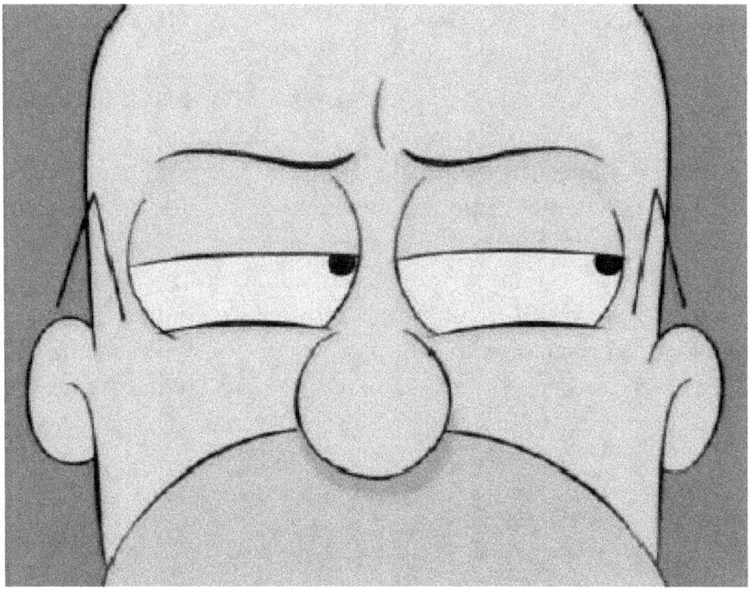

hemispheres. Remember that from before, The Stroop Effect? Ready… Set… Go!

"If it wasn't for your belly button, every morning you would wake up covered with lint."
-Lon Safko

Inspiration

Wayne Dwyer said in his March 8, 2004, PBS presentation of his "Power of Intention":

Inspiration or "inspire", originally came from the words "In-Spirited" or the Greek root of "inspiritu".

The Greeks believed that when someone is truly "inspired" or "In-Spirited" that they are touched and gifted by the Gods with that idea, that moment of "Eureka".

Ptolemy wrote that when you are inspired you are in-Spirited and you are motivated to create. When you are inspired, you are in-Spirited by some great purpose on some extraordinary project, where all of your thoughts break their bonds. Your mind transcends limitations, your consciousness expands in every direction, and you find yourself in a new, and a great, and a wonderful world. Dormant forces, forces you didn't think were accessible to you, faculties and talents come alive, and you discover yourself to be a greater person by far than, you ever dreamed yourself to be. When you are inspired you are in-Spirit."

"Change forces growth."
-Lon Safko

David by Michelangelo

Michelangelo completed the amazing marble carving in 1504 and is located in Florence, Italy. If you can ever get a chance to view it in person, it is well worth the trip and wait in line.

When Michelangelo was asked how he created his masterpiece David, he answered,

"I simply chipped away everything that wasn't David."

Please give Michelangelo's quote some thought. Many times I see the solution, then all I have to do is… create that!

"Color outside of the lines."
-Lon Safko

Archimedes' Eureka Moment

Archimedes was challenged by the King to help discover a possible theft. The King had previously commissioned a goldsmith (jeweler), the create a beautiful crown of emeralds, rubies, and gold.

Soon after, the goldsmith presented his beautiful crown to the king. The king became suspicious of the goldsmith. He thought "What if the goldsmith made a crown of pewter and plated the cheap metal with gold keeping all the remaining gold for himself?"

The problem was, how could the King test the crown without cutting it open? The process of verifying the gold content would destroy the crown itself. So, the King asked Archimedes, one of the most brilliant minds of his day for help.

Archimedes lamented over how to test the crown without destroying it forever. He looked everywhere and asked every scientist he could find. He read all the texts, and thought about it day and night.

One day he decided to take a break and a hot bath. He got the water piping hot and filled his tub to the very top. As he stepped into the water, he noticed the water was slowly pouring over the top of the tub onto the floor.

He realized the more he put his leg into the water, the more the water spilled over. This led him to realize the volume of water spilling over was exactly the same as the volume of his leg. The volume in equaled the volume out.

He further thought if he were to lower some scrap gold into a vessel filled to the top with water, he could measure the volume and weight of the water that spilled over. This would lead him to a ratio between the weight and volume of the water. He could do the same for other non-precious metals such as pewter.

He deducted after lowering the crown into a vessel of water, the water the crown displaced should have the same ratio as the scrap gold. If the weight to volume ratio was not exactly that of the pure gold, then the crown could not have been made of gold.

At that moment, as the story goes, Archimedes yelled "Eureka", jumped from the tub and ran naked through the streets of Greece. At that very moment, Archimedes had discovered Specific Gravity.

He ran to tell the King (I think a friend must have to him to at least put on some pants). After explaining what he had discovered, the King ordered the crown and the goldsmith to be brought before him. When they both arrived, the King ordered to have the crown cut in half.

When the King was presented with both halves of the gold crown, it was evident that the crown was made of pewter and only plated with the gold. The goldsmith had stolen the King's gold.

That moment was one of Archimedes greatest triumphs, a great day for science greatest discoveries, but not so much for the goldsmith. His head was cut off.

Where Do You Get Your Eureka Moments? In the hot tub or shower, the car, while exercising, walking, or listening to music. Give this some thought. Close your eyes right now and think about it.

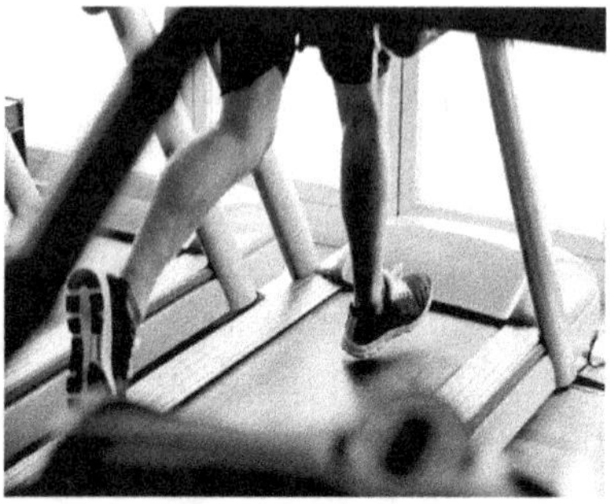

Inspiration Is Like…

Several years ago, I was interviewed by a magazine about one of my inventions and the reporter asked me what the moment of inspiration was like. Wow! I had never thought about it before. I really didn't know how to describe it.

After thinking about it for a moment, I realized it was like remembering the future. The reported pointed out that was what Merlin the Magician said, "His moments of inspiration is like remembering the future!" I wasn't familiar with the Legend of King Arthur and Merlin The Magician at the time so I took his word for it.

It's true and we do it all the time. Do you want to experience that feeling? Just remember something.

My wife and I play a game most nights where we challenge one another to remember something. The first person to remember it wins. We don't really win anything other than we prove we haven't lost our minds (or at least our memories).

It usually starts out "Who was that guy… you know… in that movie… you know… the movie with the girl, the girl with the hair, and he was… you know…" Then she'll say "Dustin Hoffman?" And I'll think to myself, "Damn… She did it again."

It really is like that. It's like remembering someone's name, a spouse's name, a date, or a telephone number. that very moment when it pops into your head is a "Eureka" moment.

Wrap your brain around that feeling and encourage yourself to have as many of these exception moments as possible. The more you embrace this feeling, the more it will happen, and the more you will remember the future.

"Four qualifications for success; training, experience, talent, and passion."
-Lon Safko

Perspective On Future / Past Innovation

Several years ago, I had lunch with Edward de Bono. He is considered one of the greatest minds on creativity and what he calls "Lateral Thinking". It was a real treat for me.

We were discussing innovation and creativity and I said "When we look back on an amazing discovery it doesn't seem to have the same wow factor as it does when we look at a current discovery."

I explained that when I discussed developing voice recognition and voice synthesizing back in the 1980s' everyone compares it to Siri and Alexa and says yeah, that's cool. "Cool?!" That was more than 30 years ago!

What if I could tell you what was going to happen in 2050? Would you be impressed? Or, what was going to happen in the year 2020. It would amaze people.

Looking back doesn't have nearly the impact as looking forward even when the innovations become part of our today's technology and culture. It's is always like "Of course you did it. Look at it today? It's obvious!"

Edward smiled and understood exactly what I was talking about. He said the perspective on innovation is like this…

Think of it as a huge tree with a lot of branches.

He said " What if I pointed to one specific leaf on that tree and asked you to trace that leaf from the leaf to the stem, to the branch, to the limb, to the trunk to the ground… How difficult would that be?"

I thought about it for a minute, trace the leaf to the ground in my head and said "Very easy. There's only one route."

He said That's right. It's no great feat. But what if I pointed to one specific leaf on the top of the tree and asked you to trace the tree from the trunk to the limb to the branch to the stem to the leaf? How easy would that be?"

I answered "Extremely difficult!'

Edward answered "Exactly. Looking back on innovation is like tracing the leaf to the ground. The path of logic is obvious. Tracing the tree from the ground to the leaf has millions of possible dead ends. It's a big deal to get that right. It's the same journey, only from a different perspective."

I froze with respect. That was an amazing insight. So much so, years later, I am sharing that private conversation with you.

Please think about that perspective of a few moments.

"Failure, just means you have to try it a different way."
-Lon Safko

What Can You Do With A Newspaper?

Give me some ideas!

Get that pad and start listing all the things you can do with a newspaper. Really! See how big a list you can make and how creative you can be!

"Don't worry, a year from now you won't even remember the details of the problem that has you worried."
-Lon Safko

Steven Wright * Birth Certificate

http://bit.ly/2zfLyhW

Here Are A Few Things You Can You Do With A Newspaper!

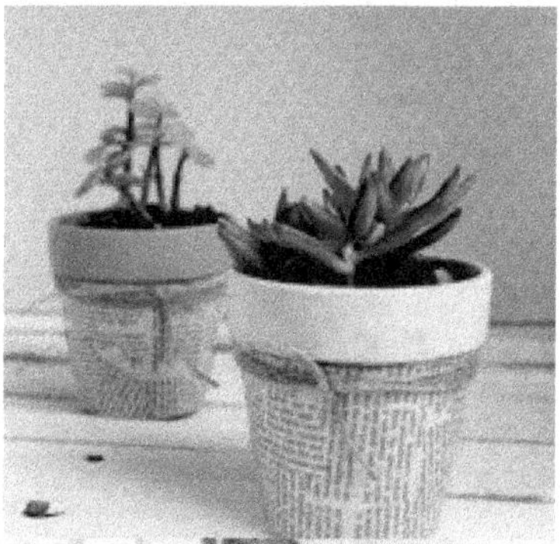

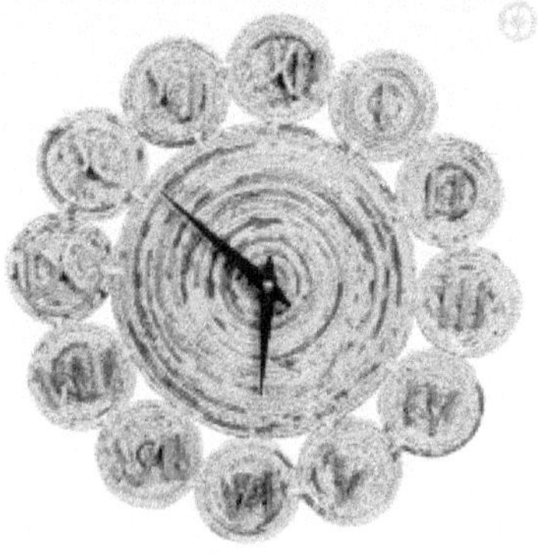

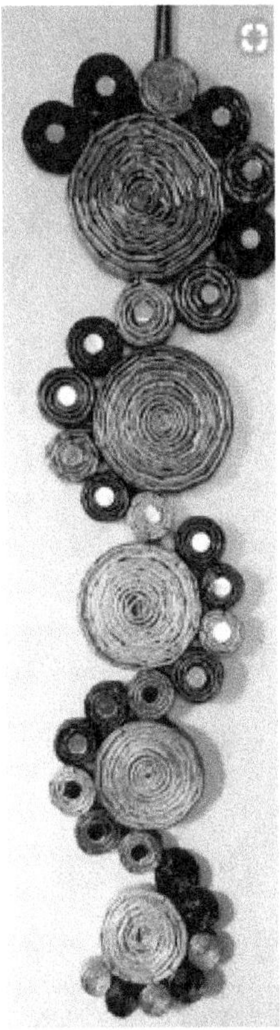

Innovation

Here's a cartoon that was given to me a while back. I thought it was worth saving and sharing. The lesson here is: Don't take

yourself too seriously.

Entrepreneur

A friend of mine was so serious about this message to me that he had it made into a brass plaque! Same lesson.

"Sometimes you just have to listen to the silence."
-Lon Safko

Inventor, Entrepreneur, Innovator

An Inventor…

Creates something new, exciting, and never before seen.

An Entrepreneur…

Builds a company around something new and exciting.

An Innovator…

Creates something new, exciting, never before seen, builds a company around it, and makes money at it.

"Sometimes if you want to know what someone is thinking, you just have to listen."
-Lon Safko

Steven Wright • Quick Sand Box

http://bit.ly/2zPQnxj

Inventor, Entrepreneur, Innovator An Inventor…

An Inventor…

Abraham Lincoln,16th President Of The United States
Was the only president to ever receive a U.S. Patent.

An Entrepreneur…

Steven Paul Jobs, Apple Computer, Inc., approximate personal net worth was: $3.3 billion at the time of his death.

An Innovator…

Thomas Edison, Innovator & Prolific Inventor 1,093 successful Patents.

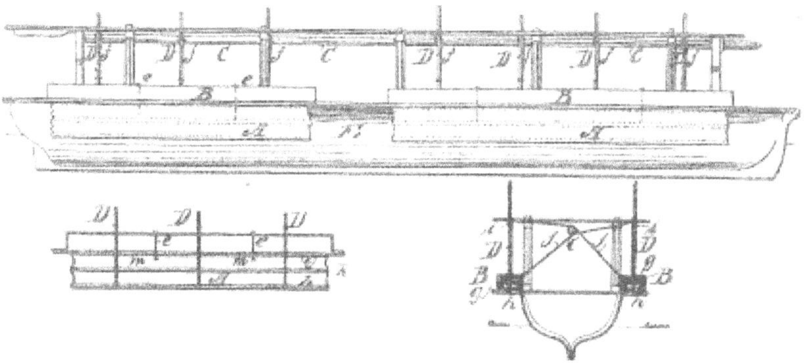

Abraham Lincoln's 1849 Patent

Think of some people you've heard or read about for each category and write them down!

"In sales, no doesn't mean no 'til there's a Restraining Order."
-Lon Safko

Mistakes Are Opportunities

The Electric Flowerpot

At the turn of the twentieth century, Russian immigrant Akiba Horowitz (AKA Conrad Hubert), was working for Joshua Lionel Cowen selling electric fans and the Electric Flowerpot. The electric Flowerpot was a flowerpot with a cylinder attached that contained a small bulb, two batteries, and a switch. You would switch on the bulb to highlight your plant.

After many failures, Hubert bought the patent for the Electric Flowerpot from Cowen threw away the pot. He sold it as the world's first flashlight. He later founded the Eveready Flashlight Company. When he died in 1928 he left $6 million to charity. Don't feel bad about Cowen, he did O.K. too.

Cowen was hired in 1901 by a Manhattan store owner to create a display to call attention to his merchandise in his window. Using his knowledge of batteries and miniature motors, Cowen designed a small electric train. It definitely worked, because the store owner returned the next day to find six orders for the window display trains. By 1902, Lionel was a toy train manufacturer. His trains continue to sell today.

Start Ideas Coming: Unleashing the Creative Mind

Creativity is simply looking at things in a different way.

Try to solve the following. The answers are on the next page. Don't cheat!

Cycle Cycle Cycle	Man Board	Stand I
R/E/A/D/I/N/G	He's/Himself	0 M.D. B.A. Ph.D.
DR. DR.	hoRN	GGES EGSG GEGS SEGG

"In my opinion, most religions are non-prophet organizations."
-Lon Safko

1. Tricycle
2. Man Overboard
3. I Understand
4. Reading Between The Lines
5. He's Beside Himself
6. 3 Degrees Below Zero
7. A Paradox
8. Little Big Horn
9. Scrambled Eggs

Necessity & Invention

Some say that necessity is the mother of invention. Sometimes that's true, but it's not. Sometimes… Invention is the mother of necessity.

Take Steve Jobs and the Macintosh, the iPod, and the iPad. Everybody seemed content with DOS (OMG!). No one said "You know what would make using a computer even better… a Mouse!"

At one point in time, no one had ever heard of the iPod or knew what an MP3 was. We all had CD's and loved them; scratches and jumps and all! The MP3 and the MP3 Player was around for several years before Steve Jobs "created" a market for an MP3 player. I owned a Philips MP3 player years before the iPod.

"Sometimes if you want to know what someone is thinking, you just have to listen."
-Lon Safko

Tool Tips

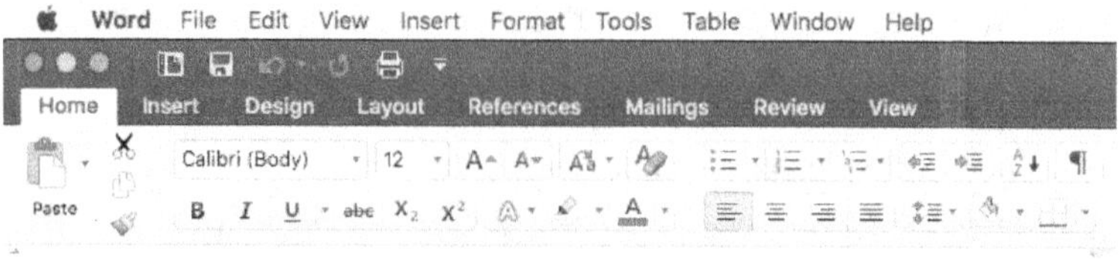

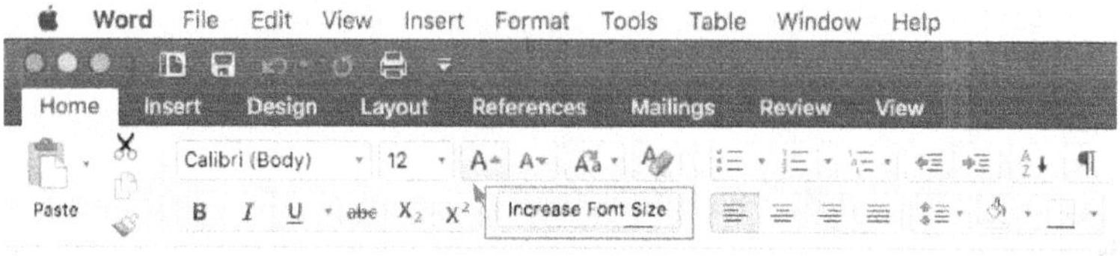

When you put your mouse cursor over a button and a window (modal) pops up to show you what that button does? That's another invention of mine from March 6, 1987, and called it "Tool Tips.

It was a "necessary" invention, while I was working with quadriplegics, I realized a quadriplegic couldn't hold a user's guide. At that time, all user's guides were paper booklets. A quad couldn't hold a book.

This idea was to help them the process of learning how to use a computer. They just had to move their head using the head-mouse to position the cursor over any button on-screen and a small window would pop up and explain the function of that button.

Just like curb cuts and ramps for the disabled, non-disabled use the convenience of them also!

During the late 1980's, Apple ~~stole, borrowed,~~ was inspired by my design and built it into their operating system. Then in 1994, Microsoft also ~~stole, borrowed~~, was inspired by Tool Tips and made it part of their operating system; Windows.

The Innovation Process

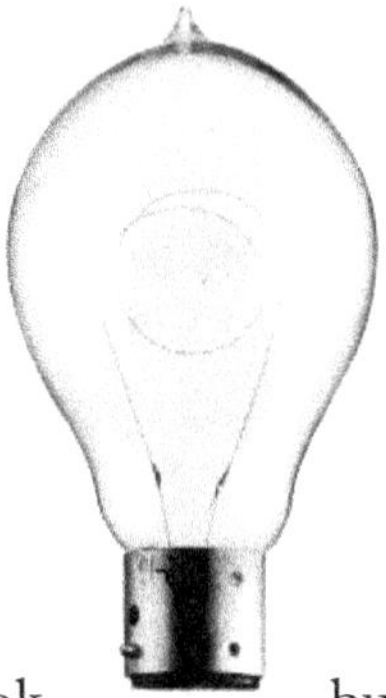

There are many processes innovators go through to get to that moment of inspiration. It does; however, come down to two major categories; Trial and Error, and what I call Intellectual Innovation.

I will share my actual process of innovation that is called The Three C's later in this book, but here's the foundational information.

Trial and Error is when an innovator just keeps trying things. He tries and tries until he has exhausted all possibilities.

Thomas Edison once said, " I haven't failed, I just found 10,000 NOT to create a light bulb."

Then there is Intellectual Innovation. This is when an innovator arrives at that moment of inspiration through a methodical process, similar to a mathematician or a physicist. They study the concept, run some numbers, list what they know and what they don't know (Convergent & Divergent Thinking (more on that later too).

Then they arrive at a solution and go test their hypothesis. If it works, the solved the problem. If it doesn't work, well… It's back to the drawing board.

"You have to be IN the game in order to win!"
-Lon Safko

Three Men And A Room

Here's a brain teaser that should keep both sides of your brain busy for some time. The problem is simple while the solution is difficult.

What we know…

Three men pay $10 each to rent a room or $30 as a group.

The clerk discovers he has overcharged the group at the group rate by $5.

He gives the bellhop the $5 to return to the three men.

The bellhop decides that $5 is too hard to divide by three and gives each man a dollar and keeps the remaining $2 for himself.

The three men have now paid $9 each, the bellhop has kept $2, making the total $29.

Where did the remaining dollar go?

Go on… Don't give up too easily. Work on it for a while.

"You can never go wrong doing the right thing!"
-Lon Safko

CHAPTER 6

INATTENTIONAL BLINDNESS

Chapter 6

Mistakes Are Opportunities

King Gillette

In 1895 King Gillette (not royalty), went to shave and found his razor to dull. As he went to the barber to have it sharpened. He stood there looking at the very edge of his razor, the idea came to him. What if I could create a "disposable blade"? No one would ever have to run to the barber and pay them to sharpen their blades.

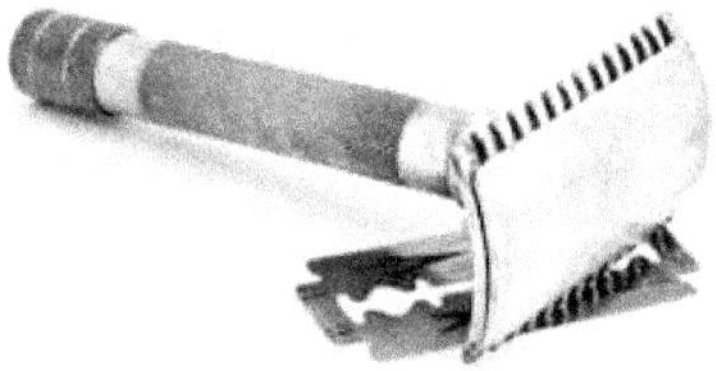

Six years of failure to manufacture the blades went by. Even MIT told Gillette to drop the project until one professor agreed to help. In 1901 the first 55, $5 razors were sold. They were very expensive for their time.

During WWI, the government bought 3.5 million razors & 36 million blades. The Gillette story has become a Harvard Business Case Study on how you can give the razor away for free or at cost, so you make huge profits on the blades.

Can you name any other similar business model?

"Capital isn't so important in business. Experience isn't so important. You can get both these things. What is important is ideas, you have the main asset you need, and there isn't any limit to what you can do with your business and your life."
–Harvey Firestone

Pattern Recognition – Bean Head

According to cognitive scientists:

- If you can find the man's head within 3 seconds, then your right brain is more developed than normal people.
- If you can find the man's head within 1 minute, then your right brain is developing normally.
- If it takes you longer than 1 minute, then your left brain is more developed than normal.
- If you still can't find it, then try looking in the lower part of the picture, between the left side and the middle.
- If you still can't find it, then I suggest you make an appointment with your optometrist.

"If not for mistakes, humans would not have evolved."
-Lon Safko

Pattern Recognition – Batman Logo

What do you see? A black swan? A Batman logo? A Ninja Throwing Star? Something else?

It's actually a big white "?" mark. If you didn't see the "?" mark at first, don't feel bad. Nearly no one does. Some people in my workshops can't see it even after being told what it is.

This happens because of our parents. It's their fault. At least that's what I tell my psychiatrist. It is kind of their fault though.

Ever since we were born, we have been taught to look for information in black on a white background. True? When was the last time you saw a white font on a black page? Never.

Newspapers, books, (this book), computer screen, canvas, nearly everything starts off white then we add black or colored information to that blank medium. So it's natural to look for the information in the black image instead of the white.

Sometimes the answers are right in front of your eyes, only you can't see them!

"Over Achieve… It's easier to delete than create."
-Lon Safko

Pattern Recognition – Two Women

What do you see here? A young woman? An old hag? It all depends on how your brain was trained to recognize patterns.
Most people see one or the other and it's difficult for them to see the other. Can you see both?

The young woman has her face turned to her right and she is looking away. The scarf and the hair are the same for both, but the chin of the old hag is the lower jaw of the young woman. The old hags mouth is the young woman's necklace. The old hag's wart on her nose is the young woman's nose. Do you see them both? Keep working on it, you will!

"I can't tolerate intolerance."
-Lon Safko

Pattern Recognition Laptop Shadows

I am going to tell you the shadowed white area is the same color as the cover. Do you believe me? I bet you don't. Look closely at it. Take your hand and cover the image below.

Hard to believe? It's amazing how much your eyes and brain will deceive you, isn't it?

"My fear of death is not that comes too early, only that it comes too late."
-Lon Safko

Pattern Recognition – Three Parked Cars

How about this image? It's obvious that the three cars are all

different sizes, right? Wrong!
How about now? They are all the same size. Damn lying brain!

"Admitting your weaknesses is your strongest strength."
-Lon Safko

The Wheels On The Bus

Let's try something different. We'll step away from the illusions and I'll show you a really simple challenge. First graders get this

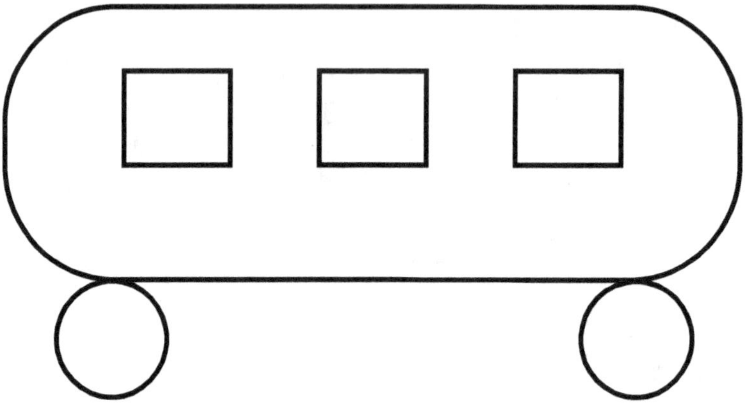

immediately. So should you.

This is a bus. Which way will the bus pull away from the curb? To the left or to the right? That's it! Grad schoolers get this right away.

ANSWER: There is only one way, the left. There is no door on this side of the bus, so the door has to be on the other side. If so, the front of the bus has to be facing left.

School kids get it because it's in their world. Somehow we grow out of that world and into one that clouds our vision and ability to see simple answers.

"Innovation: Perceiving Information Uniquely."
-Lon Safko

Do You See Black Dots

Can you count the black dots? How many black dots are there? Take your time. You will be graded on this.

You see white dots? So, there aren't any black dots? Which is it, black dots or white dots? This is a standard jpeg. It is static and does not change.

I guess you're seeing things again? As long as you're not seeing dead people, we can continue.

In the back of your eye, is your retina. The retina is made up of two types of cells; rods and cones. The rods are good for low light, low-frequency light, and black & white reception and the cones see color. both nerve endings fire when hit by an appropriate photon of light.

The light hits the cones or rods, activates the nerve and the nerve gets flooded with an electrolyte (acetylcholine) that completes the circuit for the nerve and sends an electrical impulse up the optic nerve to the vision center at the rear bottom of your brain.

Once the rod or cone nerve has been activated, the brain injects acetylcholinesterase to counteract the previous acetylcholine in preparation for the next electrical signal. This process happens 100 to 200 times per second on average. It's the amount of time for your eye to flush the electrolyte out of that nerve so it can see something new. The amount of flushing time it takes is the amount of time you still see the black dot.

As the image is mostly black, your rods see black. As your eyes move around they see the black until they have been flushed. The amount of time is different from person to person. Some people only see the dot for a millisecond, while others see it for a much longer time. Either is OK.

I show this to prove once again, you can't believe your own eyes. Sometimes you see things that aren't there and sometimes there are answers right in front of you and you physically can't see them.

Now that you know your eyes continuously play tricks on you, you can be more aware of this fact and be more cautious when looking for that next solution.

"Sincere, Authentic, & Transparent. If you're not transparent, people will see right through you."
-Lon Safko

Pattern Recognition – Elephant Legs

Now, quickly, turn the page. While sitting on the next page, did you think there was anything wrong with the elephant? Most likely not.

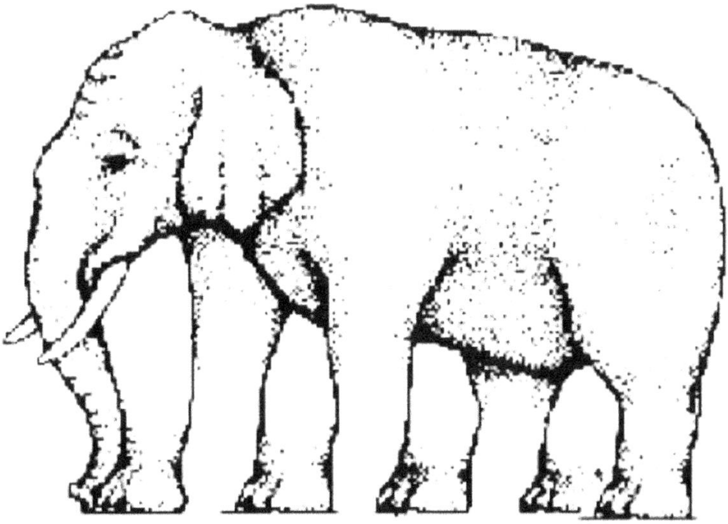

How many legs does the elephant have? Two? Too Many?

This gets back to your brain's ability to recognize patterns. We saw the elephant, our brains said OK, an elephant, and we moved on. It wasn't until I called attention to the elephant's legs did you make your brain stop telling your everything was OK with the elephant that your brain let you look at it objectively.

Recognizing patterns is a shortcut that our brains use to process information quickly based on past experience. If you are standing on a curb and a large metal rectangular object is getting bigger, your brain doesn't have to tell you it's the 5:14 Cross-Town Commuter bus, all it has to do is yell "STOP!"

"Why does mathematics give preferential treatment to even numbers? Odd x odd is odd, even x even is even, and even x odd is even."
-Lon Safko

Inattentional Blindness or Selective Attention

In this video, I will ask you to count how many times the players wearing white pass the basketball. Scan the barcode or click the link below and be very careful to count the number

of times the white shirt team passes the ball.

http://bit.ly/2hFeCnH

Go watch it now… then come back. Don't read any further. The correct number of times the ball is passed is 15; however…

Did you see the gorilla? Play the video again and this time watch for the gorilla!

Mind blown again? We were so attentive to the ball passing we didn't see the freaking gorilla walked across the screen, did a little dance, and walk off without being seen! OMG! I think my brain's broke!

This is why witnesses at the scene of a crime are so unreliable. When we remember back we didn't really see it the way it happened, and our memory manufactures the mind's video according to how we wanted to see and what we saw as compared to our past experience.

Remember the old hag and the young woman from before?

"Traditional Media, Social Media, Digital Media… TraDigital Media!"
-Lon Safko

Apollo Robbins

http://bit.ly/2hLkUSY

"If you don't fully understand marketing and sales, "If you build a better mousetrap… you just end up with more dead mice!"
-Lon Safko

Steven Wright • Powered Water

http://bit.ly/2zTIoxo

What's Behind The Bars

Do you see anybody behind the bars?

Try shaking your head from left to right while looking at the image and Imagine.

"An Intellectual is someone who can discern patterns; A Genius is someone who can discern patterns where none are obvious."
-Lon Safko

Pattern Recognition – Door Panels

Here another tricky pattern recognition activity. This is a classic door with square raised panels. Stare at the white "X" in the center of the image.

Do you see the square panels? You saw the "square panels because I told you to see them. Now I want you to see "Circular" panels.

Stare at the "X" again and think circular panels. Circles will pop up out of nowhere. Do you see them?

"Creativity requires the courage to let go of certainties."
-Erich Fromm

Pattern Recognition – Antique Jug

Take a look at this antique jug. What do you see?

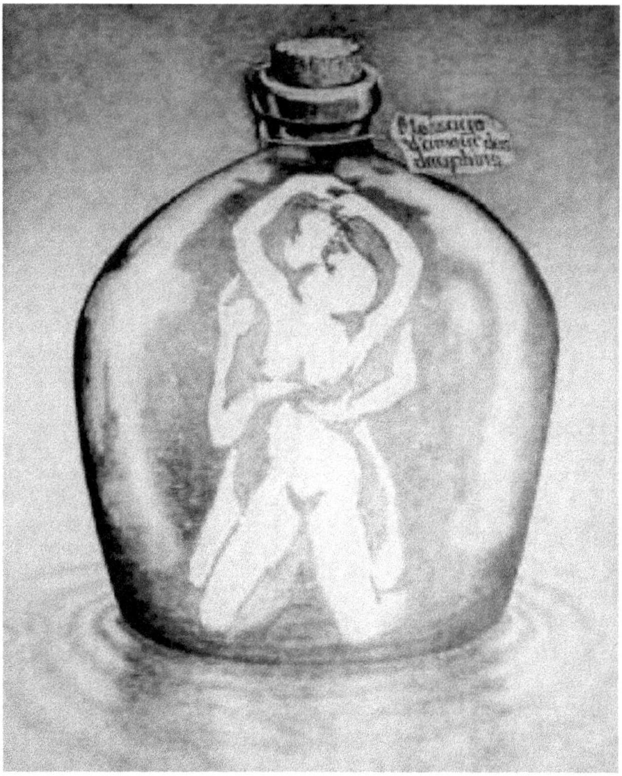

Nearly all school children see nine dolphins.

Did you see dolphins or something else? Do you have a dirty mind and see an intimate couple embracing? You don't have a dirty mind. Again, it's all about perspective. We have a much more "mature" library of patterns to draw from.

"I don't know the key to success, but the key to failure is trying to please everybody."
–Bill Cosby

Mistakes Are Opportunities

Vasoline

In 1859, Robert Cheesebrough a young chemist and pharmacist on the edge of bankruptcy, went to Titusville, PA to find success in the new oil boom.

While talking with the roughnecks he heard them complain about the pasty paraffin-like residue that clogged up the drilling rods. They added that when rubbed on a cut, the cut healed faster. This was an annoying and expensive waste product.

When he worked on purifying his petroleum jelly he used a vase he took from his wife. He then added the popular medical word ending "ine" at it became "Vaseline"!

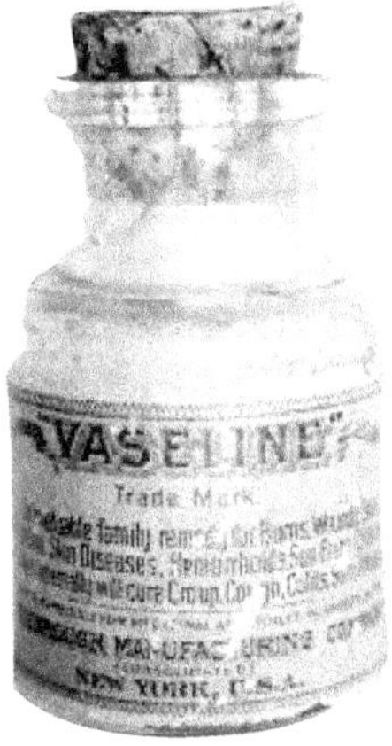

Like Dr. Joseph Lister's, Lister-ine…

Also: 3-M's Glue, Union Carbide's Ethyl Glycol, Slinky, and Weyerhaeuser's Wood Chips.

"Progress is 95 percent routine teamwork. The other five percent relies on restless, inner-directed people who are willing to upset our apple cart with new and better ideas."
–Michael LeBoeuf

CHAPTER 7

DEFINING THE BOX

Chapter 7

Defining The Box

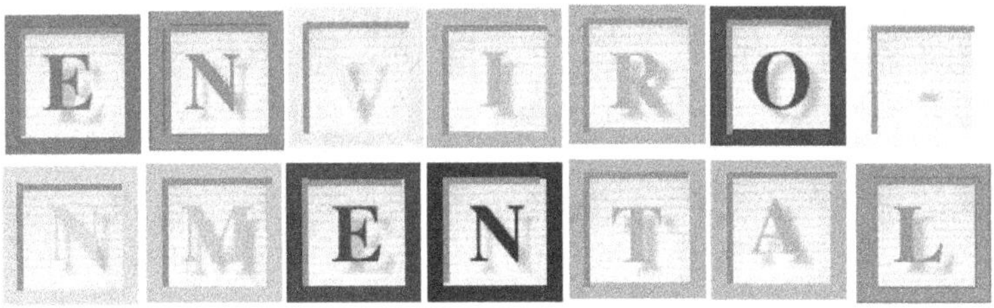

Environmental Blocks

When you are trying to be creative or innovative, there is a myriad of reasons, causes, and blocks that can prevent you. In addition to training your mind, you have to train the people around you to accept your quirkiness a necessity to act differently, say unusual things at inappropriate times, and respect your alone time to think.

All this within reason of course. Don't go acting insane and tell everyone I encouraged you to do that.

I have a hot tub. Most mornings I go to the tub just as the sun is coming up and think. I go over my tasks for the day. Write emails in my head. Design graphics. And, occasionally, solve big problems.

I also stay up late most nights and watch everything science. My wife makes a reference to the old movie "European Vacation", by calling my shows, the "cheese channel". I do have to admit, I have seen a show or two in the making of cheese.

I watch them at night after she goes to bed so she doesn't have to hear all that science. She likes her sleep and I can summarize the show the following morning.

I get up early and go to bed late. We have an understanding, I don't wake her up when I come to bed, I don't wake her up when I get up, and she respects my quiet time.

If she was concerned about my sleep habits or didn't understand why I sometimes just like to be alone with my thoughts, it would definitely be a problem for me to find the right environment to gather information and sort it out.

How many different Environmental Blocks can you think of that could prevent you from you from your quiet time to think?

Here are a few to get your brain heading in the right direction.

- Lack Of Cooperation And Trust Among Colleagues, Friends, & Family
- Bosses Value Only His Or Her Own Ideas
- Society Does Not Reward Creativity
- Ego & Insecurities
- Distractions from your Phone, Email, And other Intrusions
- Lack of time, money, expertise, and other resources
- Nowhere to work

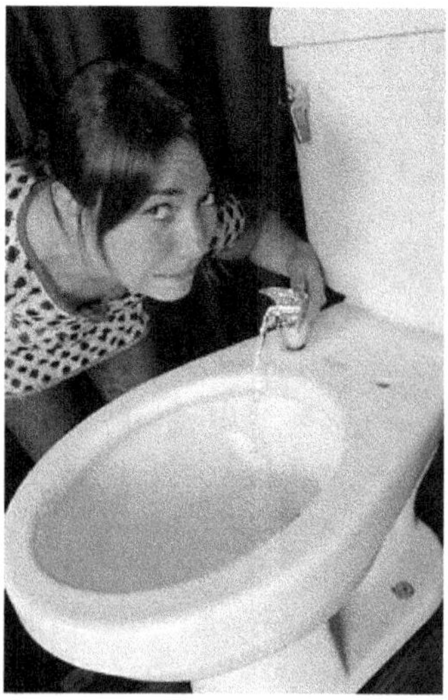

Can you think of any other Environmental factors that could prevent you from being less creative and innovative? Write them down.

"Ideas must work through the brains and the arms of good and brave men, or they are no longer better than dreams."
–Ralph Waldo Emerson

Emotional Blocks

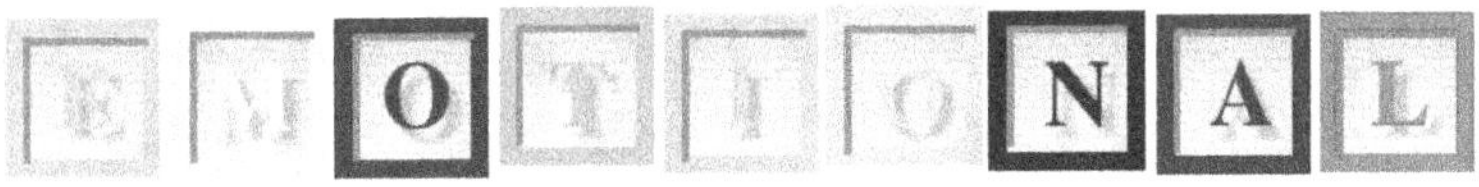

There are Emotional Blocks as well. There are reasons why we won't allow ourselves to be innovative, because of how we might look to others or how we judge ourselves.

Here is a short list of reasons we hesitate in getting into that innovative state of mind.

- ✦ Peer Pressure And Judgement
- ✦ Fear Of Failure
- ✦ Change Creates Insecurity
- ✦ Easy To Judge - Hard To Be Judged
- ✦ Not Comfortable Crossing The Line Or Getting Out Of The Box

Can you think of any other Emotional factors that could prevent you from being less creative and innovative? Write them down. Writing them down helps you to "realize" them and make them more real to you. It also reinforces your short-term memory and strengthens the neuro-pathways in your brain and make it easier to recall this information at a later date.

'We love to overlook the boundaries which we do not wish to pass."
–Samuel Johnson

Cultural Blocks

There are also many of Cultural Blocks that prevent us from being creative. Here's my starter list. Add some of your own.

- Taboos
- Fantasy And Reflection Are A Waste Of Time
- Playfulness Is For Children Only
- Problem Solving Is Serious Business, Humor Is Out Of Place
- I'm Not Supposed To Do That
- You Will Appear Immature
- Left Brain Is Good — Right Brain Is Bad
- Tradition Is Preferable To Change
- Any Problem Can Be Solved By Scientific Thinking And Lots Of Money
- Change Is Difficult - Takes Work
- You Need Both (The Engineer & The Architect)
- George Lucas Anyone?

Can you think of any other Cultural factors that could prevent you from being less creative and innovative? Write them down!

Beyond The Boundaries

Action Tip…

Left Brainers: Once a week, try something you have never done before, really.

Right Brainers: Once a day, sit quietly and think calming thoughts for 15 minutes. I know. Force yourself.

Grab your pen and paper again!

Question: Are you more like a square or a circle? Write it down.

Now, tell me why? Think of all the reasons you could justify to anyone why you are more like one over the other.

I know all you sophisticates out there think all this sounds silly and you are tempted to skip it and keep reading… Don't. These exercises really do train your brain to think differently. Stay with me on these.

"If you can't solve a problem, it's because you're playing by the rules."
–Paul Arden

Overcoming Barriers

What innovative projects have you worked on in the past where you had to deal with barriers in Environmental, Emotional, or Cultural barriers?

Think of one particular case.

How were you able to overcome those barriers?

Write a small short story explaining the barriers and how you overcame them!

"All Obstacles shall be overcome by commitment."
-Da Vinci

Getting Beyond the Boundaries

Breakthroughs in thinking require a willingness to push ourselves beyond our comfort zone. This allows us to get past "the way it has always been done."

Here's a little test to see if you are more of a "left brain thinker" or a "right brain thinker". Move quickly, write your answers down, go with the first answer that pops into your head.

1. Do you usually have a place for everything?

   a. Yes
   b. b. No

2. In thinking about your day's activities, which is most typical of your style?

   a. I make a list of all the things I need to do, people to see, etc.
   b. I just let it happen.

3. Which best describes you?

   a. I would not rely on hunches to help me make important decisions.
   b. b. I frequently have strong hunches and follow them.

4. You think of daydreaming as:

   a. A waste of time.
   b. A viable tool for planning my future.
   c.

"The only reason some people get lost in thought is because it's unfamiliar territory."
-Paul Fix

5. In a problem-solving situation, you:

a. Think about it, write down all the alternatives, arrange them according to priorities and then pick the best solution.
b. Wait to see if the situation will right itself.

6. In school, you preferred:

a. Algebra.
b. Geometry.

7. Sit in a relaxed position and clasp your hands. Which thumb is on top?

a. Your right
b. b. Your left

8. When you want to remember directions, you

a. Write notes.
b. Visualize the information.

9. In sports or performance, do you often perform better than your training and natural abilities warrant?

a. No
b. Yes

10. You learn athletics and dancing better by:

a. Learning the sequence and repeating the steps mentally.
b. Getting the feel of the music or game.

"The person who has no imaginations has no wings."
-Muhammad

Let's Total Them Up!

Add up your a's & b's.

If you answered "a", 5 or more as then you are generally a left brain thinker.

If you answered mostly b's, then you tend to be more right-brained.

The concept of right brain thinking and left brain thinking boundaries are broken when we engage the whole brain, which happens when you generate an innovative idea.

While your right brain is developing the idea, your left brain is communicating that idea and gather more information that might make that idea better.

Innovative thinking requires that we break out of our comfort zone, have fun, and be creative!

"A committee is a cul-de-sac down which ideas are lured and then quietly strangled."
-Sir Barnett Cocks

THE NINE DOTS

The Nine Dots

Here is the epitome of thinking outside of the box. In the mid-1980's when I was studying Tom Peter and his book "In Search of Excellence" I saw this exercise for innovative thinking.

It will be a great gauge for you measure the amount of innovative thinking concept you have learned so far.

Challenge 1

The rules are very simple. Start with your pad and pen. Then, drawn nine dots in a 3 x 3 configuration, like this:

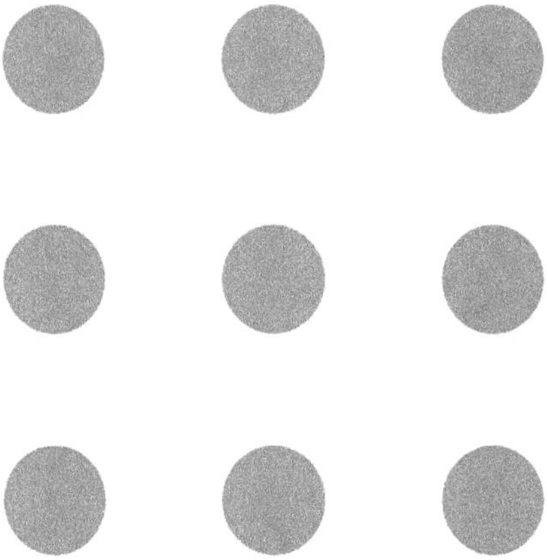

Here are the rules. Connect the all nine dots using four straight lines. That's it. Really, that's it.

And… You can't lift your pen, you can't fold the paper, none of those tricks. Just put your pen down and drag it four times; 1, 2, 3, and 4.

To create a bit of a challenge, set a timer to say 2 minutes. It should take only 30 seconds or so. Now, go! The Answer is on the next page. No peeking!

What do you think? Did you solve it in 30 seconds? 2 minutes? At all? Most likely you didn't solve it. It's tough to get out of what Joyce Meyer, the television evangelist calls stickin' thinkin'.

We have been so conditioned it's nearly impossible to see solutions right in front of our eyes.

The reason you couldn't solve this was, you put too many restrictions on your possible solutions. You made up rules that prevented you from finding the solution.

Below is how you solve this challenge.

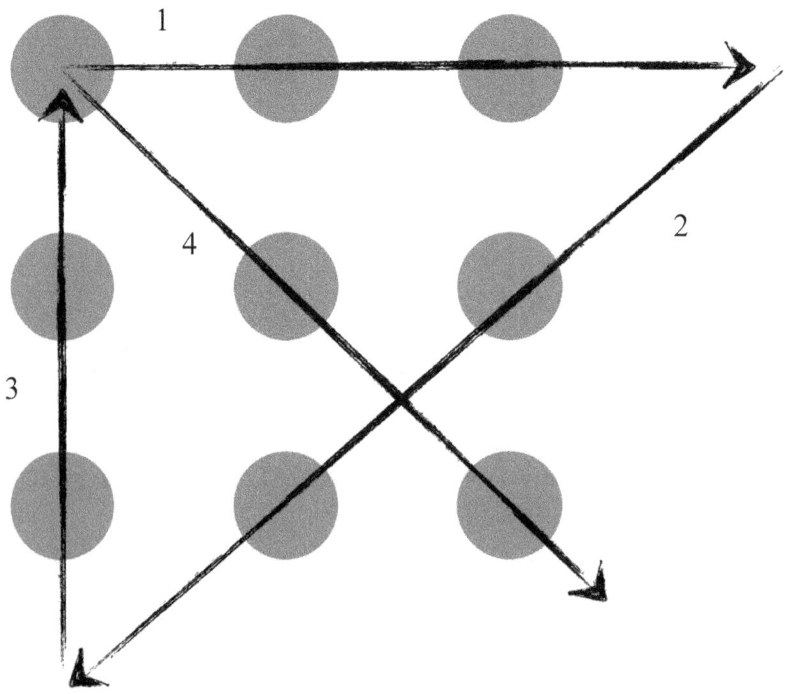

When you analyzed this problem you read the rules. You try to think your way around them such as lifting your pen, folding the paper, or not making the lines straight.

The main problem is, you made up the rule that you had to stay within the confines of the nine dots and within the imaginary box. Staying within the dots was not part of the rules.

Our conditioning by our parents, other loved ones, and people in authority taught us to stay within the lines, color within the lines, and stay inside the dots. If you want to get your creativity back, you have to break out of that box! Look at things differently and fight all those years of conditioning with everything you have.

Challenge 2

Did you think this puzzle was too difficult? OK. Take your pen and pad and draw the nine dot diagram below again. This time, connect all nine dots with only three lines. All the rules are the same. Three straight lines, can't lift your pen, can't fold the paper. Now that you know the answer, it really should take only 30 seconds to solve this; however, try to solve it in under 2 minutes. Ready, set, go!

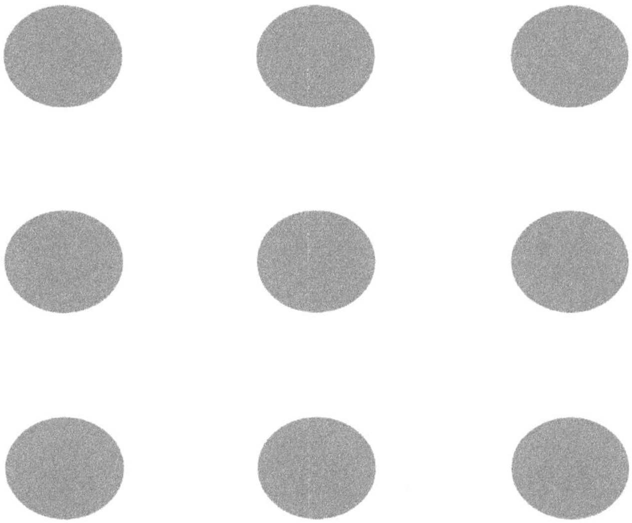

How did you do? Did you solve it quicker this time? No? Why not? Let me guess. You imposed more restrictions on your ability to solve this even though they weren't part of the rules we discussed. Right?

First. Did you draw the nine dots like the image you have seen twice before? Large round circles or did you make little tiny dots on the paper? Remember, you needed to draw the nine dot diagram like the ones shown before.

Here is the solution on the next page. Do not sneak a peek…

"If you can't make an important decision, decide to wait. You don't have enough information."
-Lon Safko

You have to first follow instructions and second, don't impose obstacles that don't exist.

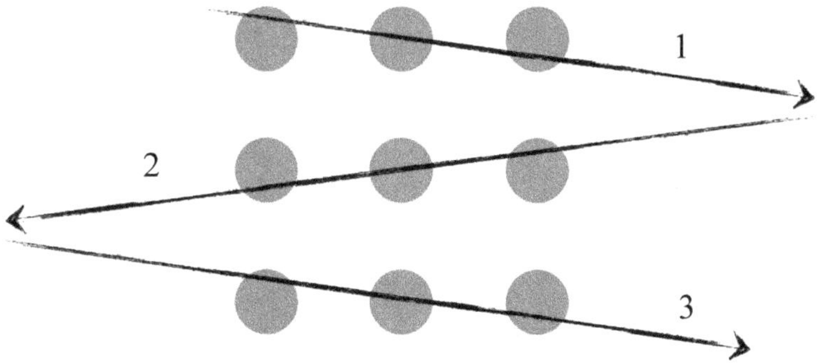

If you drew the nine dots like instructed that would have helped, but it would not have solved it for you. The stronger conditioning is to always connect the dots through tier centers. Again, that wasn't part of the rules, but I bet you did it anyway. The instruction implicitly said to only connect the dots.

Make yourself aware of all the restrictions you put on yourself every day solving everyday problems and you can eventually work around them.

Challenge 3

OK... Now, draw the nine dot diagram and... connect all nine dots with only one line. That's right. One straight line.

Ready, set, go!

I bet you didn't see that one coming! Once again, no one said the line had to be as thin as a line from a pen. Use a roller!

Don't feel bad if you didn't get the solutions. Most people don't. This is a testament to how conditioned we all really are. It's decades of being told to conform, connect the dots using the center of the dots, color inside the lines.

It's time to break out of those dots and your old habits. The fact that you purchased this book is a great indication you were aware that something happened to your creativity and you wanted to know where it went and who took it. It was mostly your parents. So, tell your therapist I said so. This way, you will have at least one legitimate reason for them screwing up your life.

CHAPTER 8

I CAN'T BELIEVE IT

Chapter 8

I Can't Believe It

If you think you work in an environment that fosters creativity & innovation, take a look at some of these quotes from individuals from companies you may recognize. It's difficult to believe what you are about to read, but all are true. It's also a wonder that these companies ever survived let alone, succeeded.

"As of tomorrow, employees will only be able to access the building using individual security cards. Pictures will be taken next Wednesday and employees will receive their cards in two weeks."
-Fred Dales at Microsoft Corp in Redmond, WA.

"What I need is a list of specific unknown problems we will encounter."
-Lykes Lines Shipping

"Email is not to be used to pass on information or data. It should be used only for company business."
-Accounting manager, Electric Boat Company

"This project is so important, we can't let things that are more important interfere with it."
-Advertising/Marketing manager, United Parcel Service

"Doing it right is no excuse for not meeting the schedule. No one will believe you solved this problem in one day! We've been working on it for months. Now, go act busy for a few weeks and I'll let you know when it's time to tell them."
-R&D Sprvsr, Minnesota Mining & Manufacturing, 3M Corp.

"My boss spent the entire weekend retyping a 25-page proposal that only needed corrections. She claims the flash drive I gave her was damaged and she couldn't edit it. The drive I gave her had a write-protect switch."
-CEO of Dell Computers

"Teamwork is a lot of people doing what I say."
-Marketing executive, Citrix Corporation

"My sister passed away and her funeral was scheduled for Monday. When I told my boss, he said she died so that I would have to miss work on the busiest day of the year. He then asked if we could change her burial to Friday. He said, "That would be better for me."
-Shipping executive, FTD Florists

"We know that communication is a problem, but the company is not going to discuss it with the employees."
-Switching supervisor, AT&T Long Lines Division

"We recently received a memo from senior management saying: "This is to inform you that a memo will be issued today regarding the subject mentioned above."
-Microsoft, Legal Affairs Division

"I have never seen a bad television program because I refuse to. God gave me a mind, and a wrist that turn things off."
-Jack Paar

The First Focus Group

http://bit.ly/2AGSF3p

"It's so much easier to suggest solutions when you don't know too much about the problem."
–Malcolm Forbes

Cut The Cake

Here's another activity. There is only one rule.

Make only three cuts and divide the cake into

eight pieces.

That's it. Take as long as you like and remember to not let convention and conditioning affect your ability to solve this problem.

The answer is on the next page.

"When written in Chinese, the word "crisis" is composed of two characters. One represents danger, and the other represents opportunity."
-John F. Kennedy

I know you tried every way you could to solve this, but I bet you never thought about cutting the cake across the middle. Why? Because you never cut a cake across the middle or have ever seen anyone else do it.

Innovation is about seeing things differently than everyone else, different than the way you are comfortable seeing them.

Here's another quick activity. Get your pad and pen and write down a few answers.

Question: If people could not see any colors, how would traffic lights be different? Write down some design ideas for a traffic light that does not rely on colors.

The first answer is easier than you could imagine. *Hint*: Look up what the 2.7 million people who are color blind do…

"It is the function of creative man to perceive and to connect the seemingly unconnected."
–William Plommer

I Can' Believe It

I could sense that you like the "I Can't Believe It" quotes, so here's a few more.

"Heavier-than-air flying machines are impossible."
-Lord Kelvin, president, Royal Society, 1895

"I think there is a world market for maybe five computers."
-Thomas Watson, chairman and founder of IBM, 1943

"There is no reason for any individual to have a computer in their home."
-Ken Olsen, president, chairman and founder of Digital Equipment Corp., 1977

"The telephone has too many shortcomings to be seriously considered as a means of communication. The device is inherently of no value to us."
-Western Union internal memo, 1876

"Airplanes are interesting toys but of no military value."
-Marshal Ferdinand Foch, French commander of Allied forces during the close of World War I, 1918

"The wireless music box has no imaginable commercial value. Who would pay for a message sent to nobody in particular?"
-David Sarnoff's associates, in response to his urgings for investment in radio in the 1920's

"Everything that can be invented has been invented."
-Charles H. Duell, Commissioner, US Office of Patents, 1899

"Who the hell wants to hear actors talk?"
-Harry M. Warner, Warner Brothers, 1927

Unbelievable!

I Can't

This is the simplest activity in the book to do, but the hardest one to follow.

1. Take a blank piece of paper and as big as you can, write the words… **"I CAN'T!"**

2. Crumple that paper up into a ball.

3. Throw it up in the air! As hard as you can!

That's it! Throw away your "I Can't!" attitude.

"Whether you think you can, or you think you can't, you're right."
Henry Ford

Mistakes Are Opportunities

Ivory Soap

In 1878 Harley Proctor while working for his father's soap and candle factory wanted to create a white, creamy, lightly scented higher end soap product. He asked his cousin James Gamble who was a chemist to help. They called it "White Soap". It sold well.

Later a factory worker went to lunch forgetting to turn off the vat mixer. When he returned, he found the soap full of air bubbles and the new soap now floated in the water. And it really sold!

Looking for a name of their new white soap, they were inspired by the forty-fifth psalm 'All thy garments smell of myrrh, and aloe, and cassia, out of the ivory palaces, whereby they have made thee glad.

When the soap was tested by a lab it was found to contain 56/100% impurities. Harley Procter flipped the findings to create "99 and 44/100% Pure!"

"You will never stub your toes standing still, but the faster you go, the more chance you have of getting somewhere."
-Charles F. Kettering

Steven Wright * Penny For Your Thoughts

http://bit.ly/2zTHTn0

CHAPTER 9

RANDOM ASSOCIATION

Chapter 9

Random Association & Innovation

This is a really fun part of the book. This section should be called "Brain Candy". For the next dozen or so page, I have presented random, fun ideas you should find interesting. So, sit back and scroll down and take a minute or so to appreciate the innovation and how you can create the same or better ideas.

As we have been discussing, many of the best ideas are simply putting two good ideas together in a way it has never been done before.

Innovation - Alexa With Eyes

The other day while listening to my playlist of music on Alexa I thought, wouldn't it be cool if you could just use your hand and swipe left and Alexa would simply go to the next tune or giving Alexa a "thumbs up" to raise the volume or a "thumbs down" to lower it? I haven't built it yet, but it would be fun!

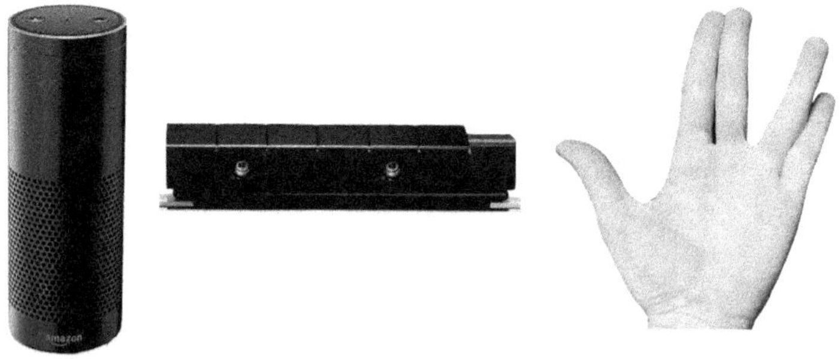

I also thought, how cool would it be to put the PS4 "Eyes" on my laptop and simply change slides by swiping left.

"All the really good ideas I ever had came to me while I was milking a cow."
-Grant Wood

Innovation - Frame-Straight

Are you tired of constantly adjusting the picture frames on your wall? Road vibrations, walking vibrations, and if you are like me, the weekly minor earthquakes knock your pictures out of level.

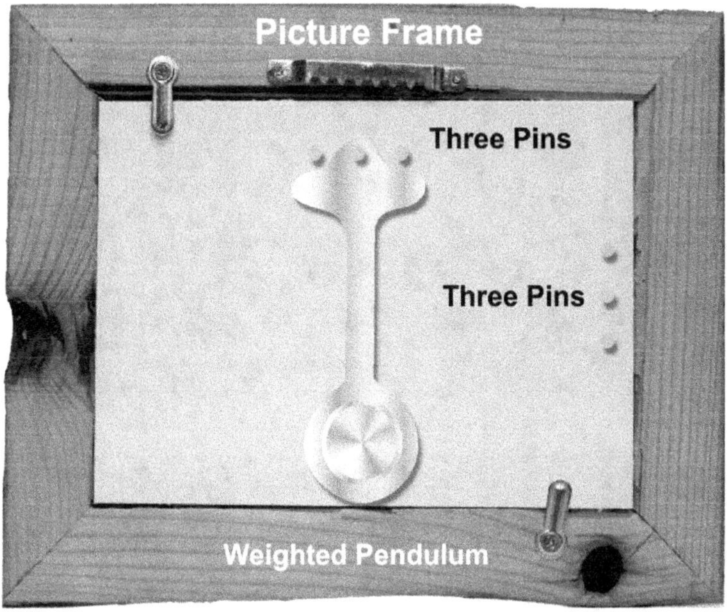

What if… There was a way to have them straighten themselves?

You could. With Frame-Straight and the addition of a simple stamped metal weighted pendulum, those vibrations can work for you. Each time it vibrates the pendulum slightly swings from side to side and straightens your frame automatically! It also works in landscape and portrait!

OK… I am not saying all these ideas is the next Pokemon Go, but they are innovative!

"The best time for planning a book is while you're doing the dishes."
-Agatha Christie

Innovation - Humidi-Vent

Problem
Is the dry winter air drying your skin? Do you find yourself moisturizing several times a day? Do you get frequent nosebleeds from the dry air? How would you solve this problem.

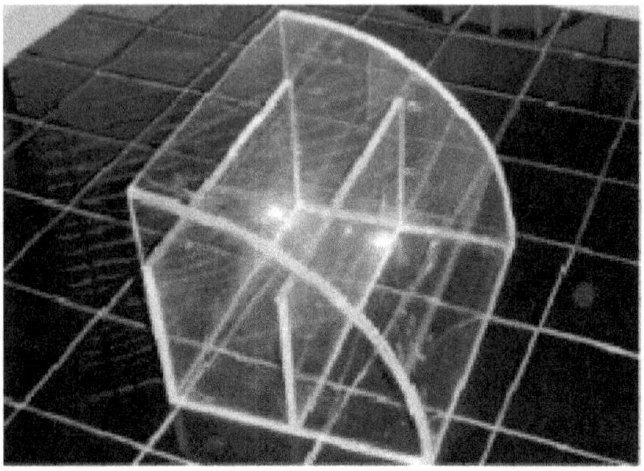

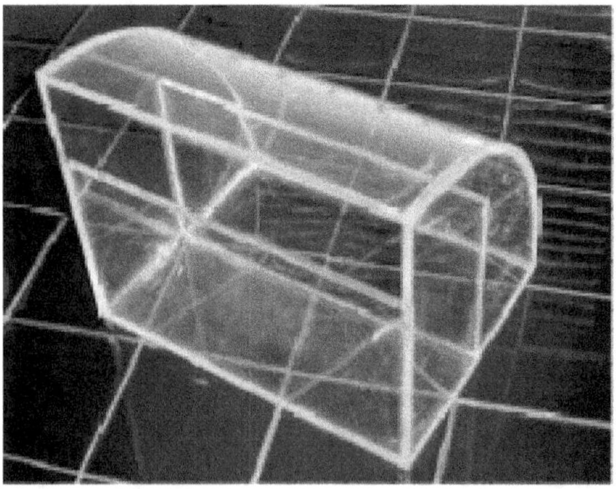

Solution
Just fill your Humidi-Vent with tap water and place it over an existing floor vent! or hang it over a wall vent and your air is fresh and moisturized.

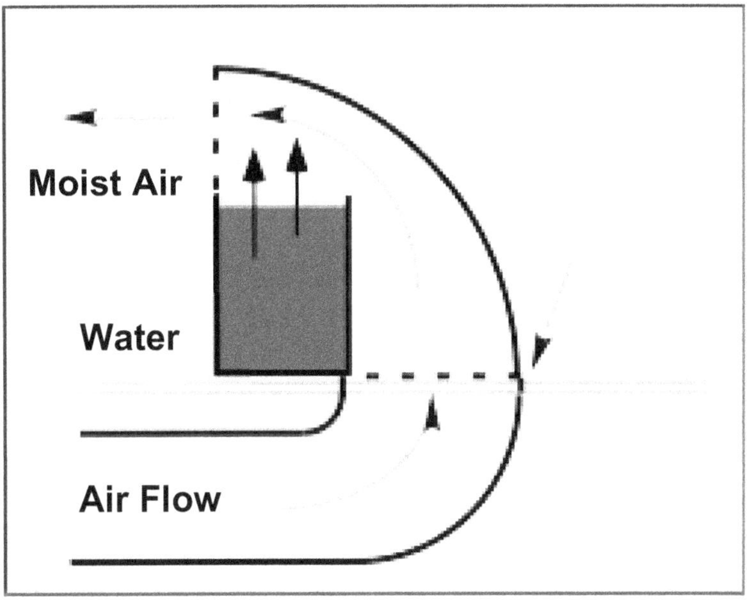

And, the clear plastic lets you know when it needs refilling.

But wait, there's more!

You can also add vanilla, cinnamon, or natural oils to keep a calming lavender, or a Christmas pine scent all year 'round!

I invented this some time ago, but never have taken the time to manufacture and sell it.

Innovation - Wet Mop Dilemma

Problem

Ever mob a floor (of course you have…) When you are finished, what do you do with the wet mop? Put it in the garage on the floor and lean the handle against the wall? Lean the wet mop head against the wall?

The mop goes sour (fill with bacteria and stink), it stains the floor and ruins the wall. Leaving the wet mop in the bucket is even worse. After a week, it really stinks!

My wife asked me to look at this and here is my solution for under one dollar.

Solution

I took a plastic pale from the 99¢ Store and cut a "V" notch in the top. I removed the handle and put one drywall screw through the back an screwed it to the wall just high enough so when the mop was placed in the bucket like the image, the handle would not touch the floor.

When we were done with the wet mop, simply hold it in the bucket and allow the handle to fall outside the V.

The mop will drip into the bucket. The mop will quickly dry before it gets stinky sour and the water in the bucket will also quickly evaporate.

No more stains, no smelly wet mops, all for under $1.

Innovation - Leaf-Caddy

Problem
If you ever raked leaves, trimmed trees, trimmed bushes, or cut grass, then you know the difficulty in picking up yard debris and leaves and carrying them to the trash bin?

Even dragging larger brush can be a time consuming job as you can only pull one branch with each hand.

Solution
With Leaf-Caddy, you need only a threaded hook, piece of scrap wood, and a tarp to make your very own Leaf-Caddy solution!

You can also hook all four corners and not sill any leaves!

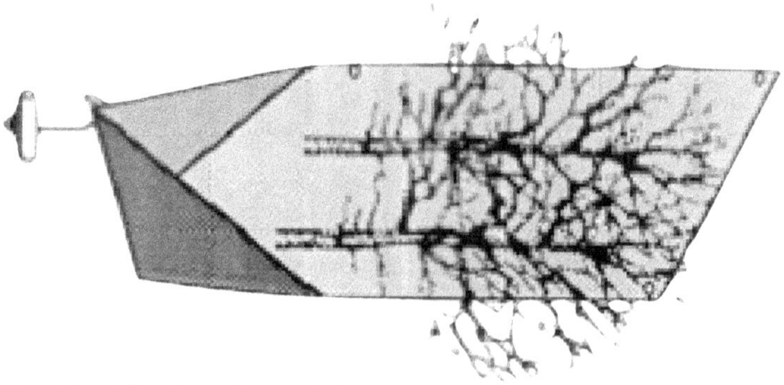

Innovation - Outback Steakhouse Earrings

Problem

When my youngest daughter was working her way through college, she worked at the Outback Steakhouse Restaurant as a hostess, waitress, and bartender. It was at the time "dangly" and "hooped" earrings were in style. Being a college girl and working for tips, she was to be stylish.

One evening she wore a tasteful but ornate pair of earrings, they actually touched her shoulder. I thought they were cool! Her boss thought otherwise. She was reminded of the restaurant's earring policy "No Earrings Larger than Quarter" and was told that either the earrings go or she goes.

Solution

So, I made her these. "No larger than a quarter." They are exactly one quarter! She wore them and almost got fired anyway. Oh well, no sense of humor.

"When you come to a roadblock, take a detour."
-Mary Kay Ash

Innovation - The Round Peg In A Square Hole

You might have noticed the image on the cover of the book. It is the proverbial "round peg in a square hole."

Problem
Several years ago, when I was explaining to someone about not being a very good employee since I always argued, never followed the rules, and saw things completely different than all the other employees, he jokingly said to me 'You fit in like a round peg in a square hole!"

Solution
I thought about his comment of "not fitting in" and the metaphor he used and one day, I came up with this. The original was made out of wood, I then had them cast in Lucite.
A "round peg does fit in a square hole!"

"To ask the hard question is simple."
-W.H. Auden

Innovation - Fish Tank Fountains

Problem
A lot of people love their fish tanks. I do too! I have had a fish tank in my office since 1990. Not the same fish of course, but a tank none the less.

I know a lot of people love tabletop water fountains. I have had my share of them also. There is something about the sound of the trickling water (white noise) that is soothing.

Solution
So, if we all agree to this, then why hasn't anyone combined a tabletop fountain and a fish tank?

The water is already the there. The pumps are there. Then why not combine them? This is called "Random Association".

"What is now proved was once only imagined."
-William Blake

Innovation - Thermo-Car

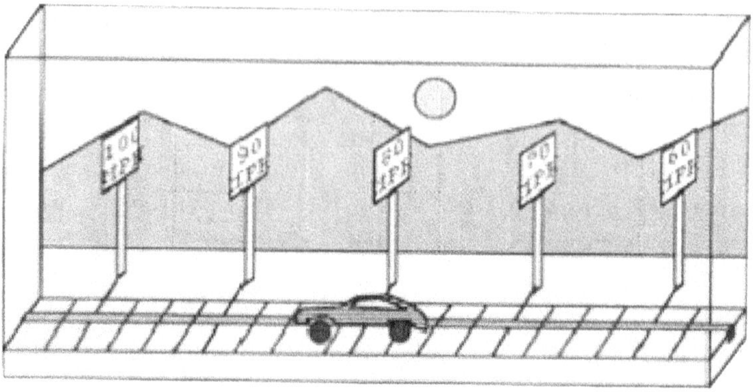

Problem

Thermometers are boring. They usually consist of a 10" glass tube filled with a red liquid or most always they are digital showing only a two-digit number on a gray quartz display. Why not have fun with thermometers?

Solution

With Thermo-Car you can watch your car race (well, not exactly race), towards the finish line or watch as your hot air balloon rises and falls with the daily temperature. Your favorite quarterback can make that winning touchdown or watch an airplane fly over the Alps!

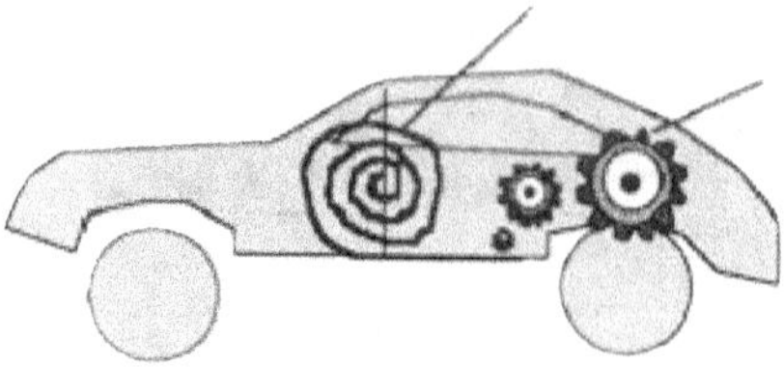

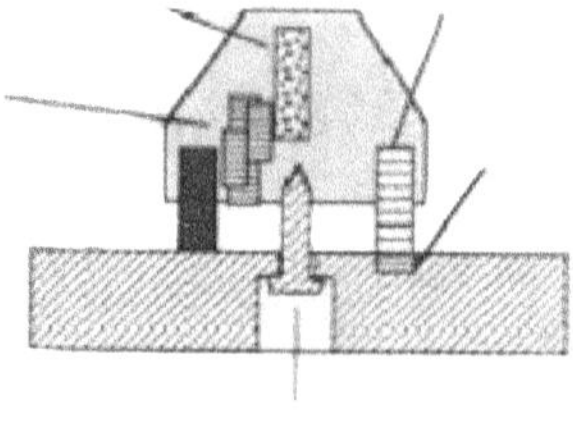

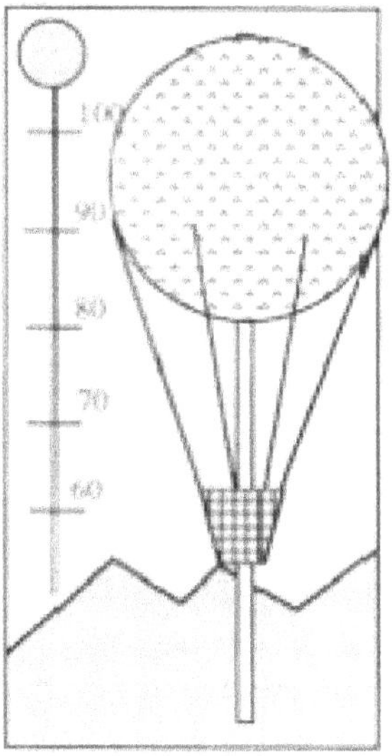

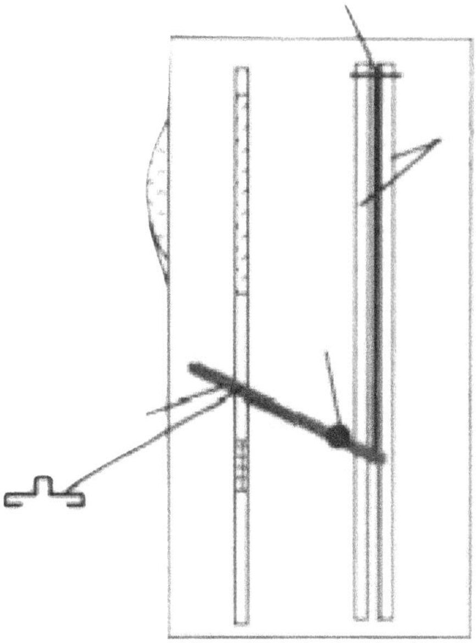

By using the heat sensitive metal Nitinol, which expands and contracts with temperature changes, any object can be moved vertically or horizontally for a dramatic and fun effect.

P.S.: Did anyone recognize the images? How and when they were created? If you did, you'd recognize that they were drawn with the earliest of Macintosh computers. So early that it was actually before color!

"Life is trying things to see if they work."
-Ray Bradbury

Innovation- Trash Can Liner Retainer

Problem

We all have been here. You put the trash can liner into the can and it's too big. So, you fold it over and hope for the best. Then the first time you throw an apple core in the can, the apple hits the bottom of the can pulling the remainder of the bag into the can. Them you have to reach in and fish it out only to fold it over until the next time.

Trash bags are made to fit loose. Otherwise, you couldn't pull them down over the rim of the can. What if you could make every can liner fit every can? (You know there's an answer coming here…)

Solution
Just loop several rubber bands around one another and fasten the two ends with a paperclip. That's it!

When the rubber bands get old and break, you're not far from the trash can, throw them in and grab a few more rubber bands and Voila!

That's Wa-La to everyone who doesn't read French, meaning "There it is!" :o)

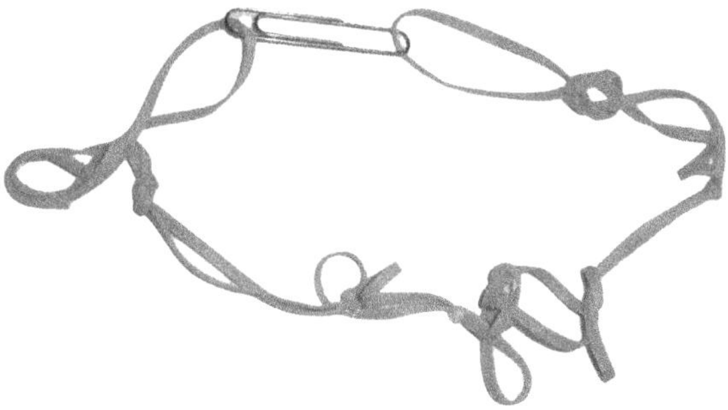

"Whenever man comes up with a better mousetrap, nature immediately comes up with a better mouse."
-James Carswell

Innovation - Shower Head Attachments

Just a reminder, this is still called Random Association. The art of taking random, everyday items and putting them together in a different way.

Problem

Have you ever stood in the shower with the shower wand in one hand and the soap in the other wishing you had a third hand to scrub with?

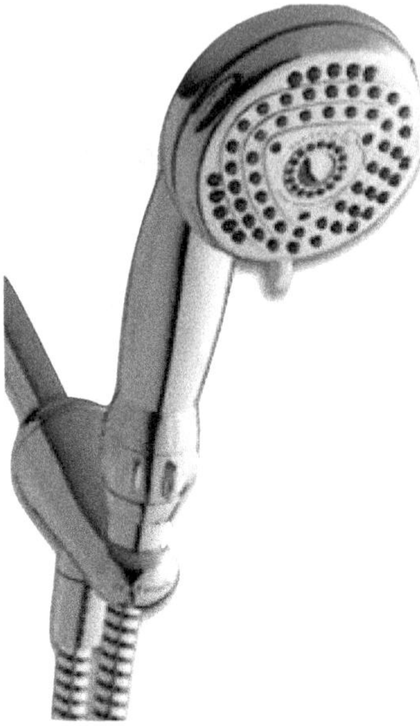

Most of us today have shower wands. I love mine. It's great for rinsing your underarms and other hard to reach places, which I am not going to list here. Once you have soaped up, washing the soap off with just running water takes time. You have to rub it a bit.

Solution

Wouldn't it great if you had a brush with running water? Or, a luffa? Or even massaging fingers for your scalp?

Why not make it so attachments, similar to vacuum attachments could just snap on and off?

Now, that would be cool.

Innovation - Inflatable Highway Safety Cones

Problem

I know you've seen those little triangle warning reflectors that disabled truck set up along the side of the highway when they break down. If you have, you've also seen half or more of them blown over by other passing trucks.

Last year my wife's car broke down and I thought about what kind of warning devices I could make for her that had to be; small, so she could carry them in her trunk, lightweight, because she would have to deploy them, cheap, so they had mass-market appeal, reflective, and couldn't be blown over.

Solution

So, I came up with Inflatable Highway Safety Cones! Do you remember the "punch-a-clown" toy from when you were a kid? You would inflate it and every time you punched it, it would fall over and bounce back up? Well…

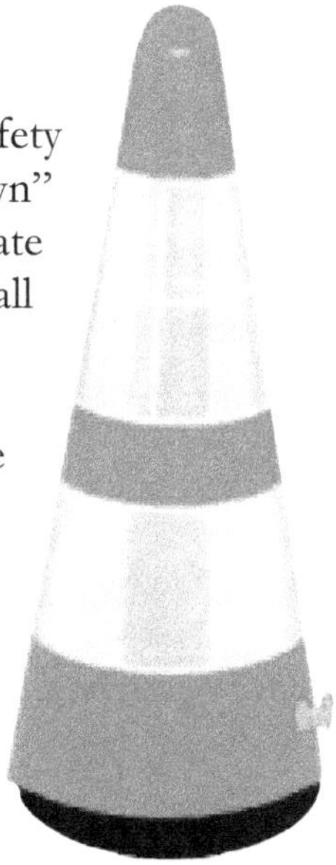

A little PVC plastic, a valve stem, and a little sand in the bottom and you have a traffic safety device that meets all of the above criteria!

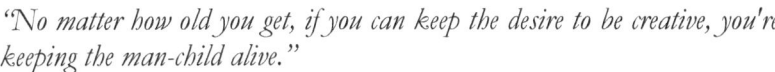

"No matter how old you get, if you can keep the desire to be creative, you're keeping the man-child alive."
-John Cassavetes

Food Hacks

Grilled Cheese Sandwich

Let me slip in a couple of food hacks here. I want you to think differently about how to do things. I am encouraging you to think differently about everything! You can do this! It's easy once you practice it!

Let's start with the traditional Grilled Cheese Sandwich. Everybody's favorite comfort food. Seriously, who doesn't love a hot bowl of tomato soup and an American cheese, perfectly

grilled cheese sandwich on a cold winter day?

I'll be right back. I am going to make one now.

OK… I am back. That was really good!

Problem

However, if you've ever attempted to make the perfect grilled cheese, you know it's always burnt on the outside and cold on the inside. the cheese is never melted or the bread is burnt. That's because you keep making it the way you mother showed you. She messed you up!

Solution

Let's take a close look at what makes a great grilled cheese good. You want the bread to be crispy and the cheese to be hot and melty. Let's start with the bread.

What you really want is the sugars in the bread to "caramelize". It's the heating of the sugars that cause that crispy crunch and dark color. Oh yeah, a ton of butter also helps add to the flavor.

Just Ask Paula Deen about butter.

So how do you get the caramelization, which doesn't take long, but still transfer enough heat to the center, enough to melt the cheese? Cook them separately. Have you ever heard of Texas Toast? It's where you make the toast on a griddle, not under heat.

To make the perfect grilled cheese, take the two slices of bread, butter one side and place them butter side down in an iron skillet. You can cook that nearly as hot as you like. I cook mine on "4". Check it from time to time and bring it to that perfect brown texture and taste.

Once browned (caramelized), take one slice and put it brown side down on a plate., add your cheese, now place the remaining slice on top, brown side up. Place that in the microwave for 30 to 45 seconds and when you open the door… You have a perfect grilled cheese! Sandwich!

Try it yourself and let me know if you can tell the difference. If you think outside of the bread, you will never burn a grilled cheese again.

One of my favorite Taco Bell commercials they have done is the talking Chihuahua. It's was one of my favorite and I never gave it a thought about being offensive. I thought he was cool.

One of Taco Bell's advertising campaigns was "Think Outside Of The Bun". I love it! If you look at nearly every fast food restaurant on earth, their main food source is always severed on a bun; McDonald's, Burger King, Wendy's, Jack-in-the-Box, Carl's Jr., all of them. With undisclosed meat on a bun.

Taco Bell appealed to those who wanted something different from the same old fast food. They needed a way to differentiate themselves from the competition. The thing that made them completely different, was there's never a bun. You got to love those Madison Avenue types! I don't hear the campaign anymore. It must have offended someone with big buns and they were forced to remove it.

I also liked their "Tacos In The Bank!" slogan. It was a good metaphor for investing in the future. Anytime something doesn't work for me, I just say "Tacos In The Bank!", because I know it will pay off someday.

The Hot Dog

As we are talking so much about food, let me give you one other simple food hack, the hot dog. Again, one of my favorite foods. I know… Please don't send me hate-emails if you a vegetarian, vegan, with PETA, care about the Ozone, or my health. I only eat the one a month or so.

I like mustard and relish on my hot dog and sauerkraut if it's available. By the way… Never put ketchup on a hot dog. Since I was born and raised near New York City we all know you never put ketchup on a hot dog is "unAmerican". And by the way, it's spelled Ketchup, not Catsup. It's been spelled Ketchup since 1711. :o)

Problem
Here's the deal. You start with the hot dog bun…

Sidebar: I still don't have a good answer as to why hot dog buns come in packs of 8, while hot dogs sell in packs of 10. You would have to cook 40 hot dogs to make that come out even.

Solution

If you build a hot dog the way everyone else does and has done, you start with the bun and place the hot dog in the bottom of the bun. then, you pile on the ingredients. As you try to take your first bite, most of the ingredients fall off the hot dog and is now running down the front of your shirt and into your lap. Not a good look.

It's like to old joke when the man goes into the doctor's office and says "Doctor, it hurts when I do this." And the doctor answers "Then stop doing that!"

If you want a delicious hot dog that doesn't end up in your lap, build it upside down. That's right, upside down. Start with your bun then place your sauerkraut in the bottom of the bun, then your mustard, then your relish. Now, add your hot dog.

By building the hot dog upside down, the meat holds the rest of the sloppy stuff in the bun! The only spilling you have to watch out for is the one end not in your mouth.

"No idea is so outlandish that it should not be considered with a searching but at the same time a steady eye."
-Winston Churchill

Innovation - The Garden Hose Dilemma

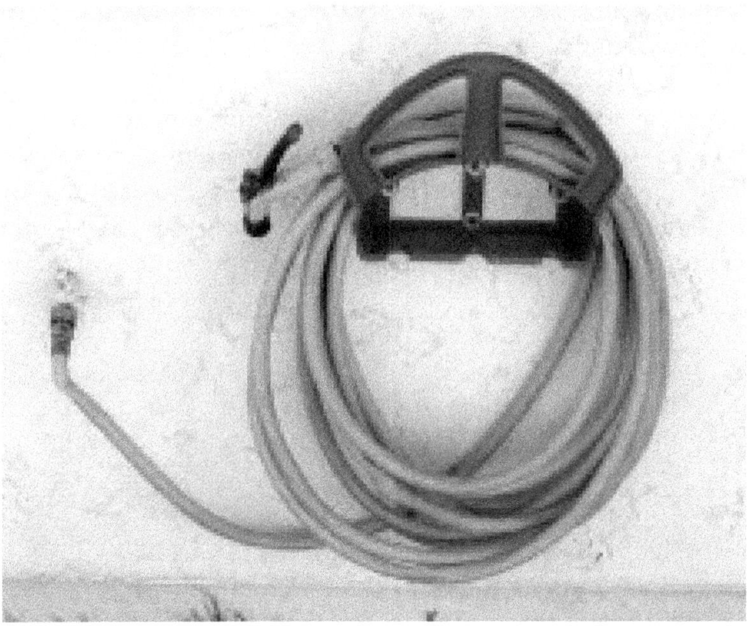

Here's a simple problem we all have had and can be easily solved if we are willing to break convention.

Problem

We've all experienced the frustration of trying to use a garden hose, only to have it twist gnarl, kink, and tangle. It seems no matter what we do, we can't keep the hose from tangling up. They even make special garden hoses called non-kinking.

Solution

You might be surprised when I tell you the reason the hose kinks is because of you. You make the hose unusable. The hose kinks and twists, because you put the twists in the hose when you store it away.

Think about it. When you put your hose away, you stand there and twist it and twist it and twist to get it coiled up all nice and neat on it little hose caddy. If you don't want the hose to wist, then… Don't twist it!

If you take a different approach and deviate from convention, you can make your hose more usable with a lot less frustration. Here's how to fix your problem.

Stretch out your hose on the lawn. Take your time to remove all the kinks and twists. Once the hose is straight, turn the water on and let the pressure straighten out the hose even more. Remove any additional twists best done when the hose is warm as it is more pliable). Turn off the water and open your sprayer to remove any

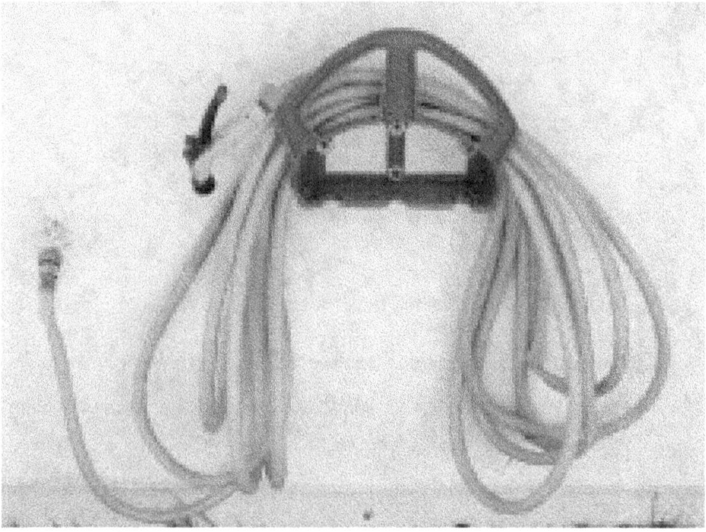

remaining water pressure in the hose. Now…
Drape your hose over its caddy, don't twist it. It won't look as pretty as your neighbors, but it won't twist either.

Solving problems are about identifying the problem and looking for simple ways to overcome the cause. I am sharing these ideas because I want to convince you most solutions are easy and right in front of your face. All you have to do is look at each problem differently. And, once you learn how, you will be able to do it with ease.

"Music is the art of thinking with sounds."
-Jules Combarie

Innovation - Leaf Bag Dilemma

Let's look at another trash bag issue this time with leaf and yard debris bags. Let's start by defining the problem.

Problem
You place the bag inside your trash can so the can will give it shape and hold it up and open. So far, so good.

As soon as you start pushing branches, sticks or prickly palm fronds into the bag, the pointy sticks tear into the bag and rip it open. It gets worse when you try to stuff the debris into the bag to compact to get more in the bag. It really rips to shreds.

Solution
So, if the problem is the stickers and sticks coming into contact with the bag causing it to rip, then don't let the sticks come into contact with the bag! Sound simple? Try this shown below.

Get a trash can and cut the bottom off it. Then, instead of placing your trash bag "inside" the can, pull it up and over the "outside" of the can.

A couple of things happen here. By doing this, you prevent the sticks and sticker from coming in contact with the bag causing it to tear. You can compress the trash even to the point of standing on it as the sticks will be pressed against the hard plastic trash can. And, because the bottom of the can is larger than the top, the trash can lifts easily out of the compacted debris.

Simply pull the trash can up and out of the leaf bag, tie it off, and take it to the curb.

Again, it's about looking at the problem differently. In this solution, we turned the trash can upside down, we cut off the bottom, and we put the trash bag on the outside of the can. It's not rocket science here. You can do it!

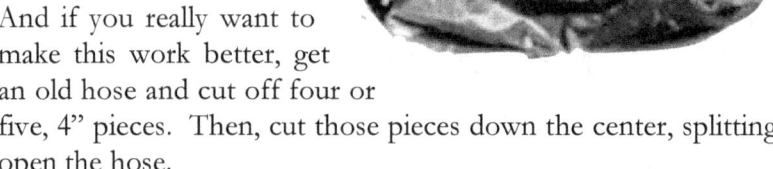

And if you really want to make this work better, get an old hose and cut off four or five, 4" pieces. Then, cut those pieces down the center, splitting open the hose.

Pull the trash bag up over the rim of the modified trash can and press the hose segments down over the rim and bag, holding the trash bag in place.

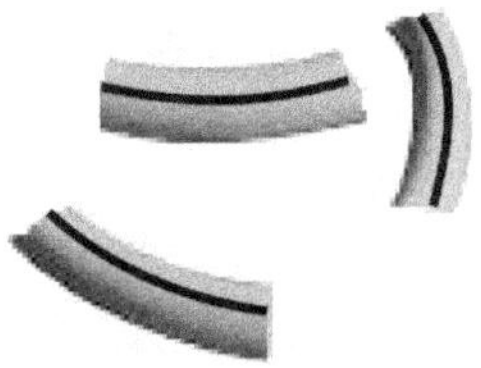

"I was taught that the way of progress is neither swift nor easy."
-Marie Curie

Innovation - Leaning Tower Of Pisa

Here's an innovative solution that is really out of the box. I tried to introduce it to the Italian government, but bogged down in bureaucracy and indifference then finally gave up. I still am sure it will work.

Problem

The learning Tower of Pisa is a spectacular monument and it really is leaning. A few years ago I got to see it in person and take the photograph below.

The tower is currently at the maximum angle it can lean. If it moves any further, it will topple. The problem is the soil it was constructed on. At one time that plaza around and beneath the tower was a swamp. Over many years, the locals dumped materials into the swamp and eventually created usable land. Unfortunately for the tower, the land wasn't structurally sound.

Once the tower was complete, its weight compacted the wet soil below causing the right side (as seen in this photo), the compress, while the left side remained in place.

The problem is wet, un-compacted, structurally unsound soil.

Solution

In the 1980's, I worked for the United States Department of Energy developing a world's first artificial intelligence computer system for the Hanford Nuclear facility. Two of the engineers I asked to join my team were Debbie & Ken Iwatate, who recently invented the process of In-Situ Vitrification.

In-Situ Vitrification was developed to safely dispose of nuclear waste. The process is pretty cool! You dig a huge pit in the ground, say 40' by 40'. Dump the waste; nuclear, medical, bio, industrial, into the pit. Cover it with sand. Place several, very large copper rods (the size of telephone poles), at each corner, and zap it with thousands of volts of electricity until the sand melts.

When it cools, it turns into a solid brick of glass. Even though it contains nuclear waste, you can safely stack them anywhere. Cool huh?

So, what if you took this process and glassified the soil beneath the Tower of Pisa? The soil would become hard as glass when it cools. Jack up the low side of the Tower and pump in some concrete. When the concrete cures, let down the jacks.

I know this innovation wouldn't be at the top of one's mind to most folks, but the process is. Looking for a solution in a completely different place. No one would think a solution for fixing the Leaning Tower of Pisa could be found on the Hanford Nuclear Reservation.

It's about random association again and you can do it!

P.S.: I'd sure like to try this someday! :o)

Innovation - Real Estate Business Card

Problem

Here's another simple innovation. A realtor friend of mine asked if I could create something to help with clients he meets to be reminded of him when they were ready to buy a house. The problem is, he meets a lot of people who are thinking of buying, but by the time they are ready, they have lost or misplaced his business card then sign with a different realtor.

Solution

This was solved by asking what's important to a buyer? The only question they have is how much house can we afford? At today's interest rate, how expensive of a house can we buy and what would the monthly payments be? So, I created this.

It's a simple table with a variety of interest rates in the left column and home prices across the top. It was printed on the back of his business card. This way, whenever a client saw a house they thought they would like to buy, they looked at the interest rate, then looked at the mortgage amount, and… There was the monthly payment.

See below.

The realtor told me recently a client who called him after 10 years! For ten years the client kept that card (the table) in his wallet.

See… Simple solutions to everyday problems.

"It is better to have enough ideas for some of them to be wrong than to be always right by having no ideas at all. "
-Edward de Bono

%	$250k	$300k	$350k	$400k	$450k	$500k	$550k	$600k	$650k	$700k
3	$1,054	$1,265	$1,476	$1,686	$1,897	$2,108	$2,319	$2,530	$2,740	$2,951
3.5	$1,123	$1,347	$1,572	$1,796	$2,021	$2,245	$2,470	$2,694	$2,919	$3,143
4	$1,194	$1,432	$1,671	$1,910	$2,148	$2,387	$2,626	$2,864	$3,103	$3,342
4.5	$1,267	$1,520	$1,773	$2,027	$2,280	$2,533	$2,787	$3,040	$3,293	$3,547
5	$1,342	$1,610	$1,879	$2,147	$2,416	$2,684	$2,953	$3,221	$3,489	$3,758
5.5	$1,419	$1,703	$1,987	$2,271	$2,555	$2,839	$3,123	$3,407	$3,691	$3,975
6	$1,499	$1,799	$2,098	$2,398	$2,698	$2,998	$3,298	$3,597	$3,897	$4,197
6.5	$1,580	$1,896	$2,212	$2,528	$2,844	$3,160	$3,476	$3,792	$4,108	$4,424
7	$1,663	$1,996	$2,329	$2,661	$2,994	$3,327	$3,659	$3,992	$4,324	$4,657
7.5	$1,748	$2,098	$2,447	$2,797	$3,146	$3,496	$3,846	$4,195	$4,545	$4,895
8	$1,834	$2,201	$2,568	$2,935	$3,302	$3,669	$4,036	$4,403	$4,769	$5,136
8.5	$1,922	$2,307	$2,691	$3,076	$3,460	$3,845	$4,229	$4,613	$4,998	$5,382
9	$2,012	$2,414	$2,816	$3,218	$3,621	$4,023	$4,425	$4,828	$5,230	$5,632
9.5	$2,102	$2,523	$2,943	$3,363	$3,784	$4,204	$4,625	$5,045	$5,466	$5,886

Innovation - Plant-Pops

Problem
How about this one? Do you have a lot of houseplants that need to be watered every few days? Are you tired of waiting for the water to filter into your potted plants? Do you have to mix separate plant food for each different kind of plant?

Solution
Then give them a plant pop. Just stick a stick in your pot and walk away! As it melts, it automatically waters and fertilizes your plants, slowly! Plant-Pops feed your plants the nutrients they need. And, they are available in different formulas for different plants! Just add food color to you mix to identify different fertilizers for different plants.

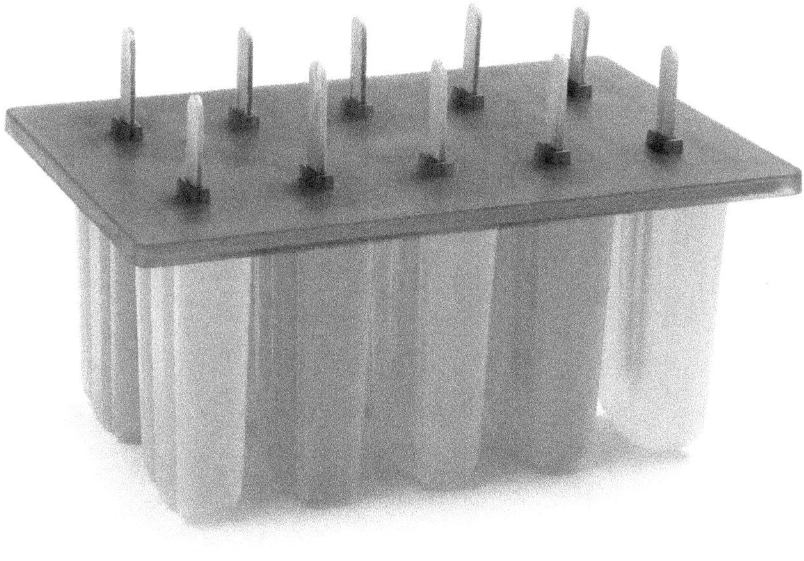

"Intelligence is something we are born with. Thinking is a skill that must be learned."
-Edward de Bono

Steven Wright • Foot Up All Night

http://bit.ly/2hJOko1

An Actual Product

This idea came full circle and formed a company out of it. The company has been in business since 1999, nearly 20 years.

Problem
This idea formed while I was a marketing director for the Port of San Diego and San Diego International Airport. The problem was their public image and their interaction with the Port. Even though they owned and managed 16 parks, including all of the hotels, museums, shops, and marinas along the 21 miles of San Diego Bay from Tijuana to Point Loma, no one knew who they were or cared.

I was asked to create a publicity campaign to attract more attention to the Port and put them in a good light. And oh, by the way, I had no staff and no budget to do this.

I thought about it for a while and realized that they weren't missing the businesses or Navy. They interacted a great deal every day. I determined that they were missing families.

After working with Apple in the mid-1980's I understood Steve Jobs idea of putting computers in the elementary schools so when the kids got to middle and high school, they would expect Apple computers. And, when they entered the workforce, it would be Apple Computers they would want.

I also understood how McDonald's differentiated themselves from all the other fast food restaurants by providing the kids habitrails, the tubes the kids played in. Great idea! When my daughter was young and had a choice of fast food for lunch, she would always pick McDonald's because of their play gyms. I liked it too because I could bring a book and get an hour with little interruption.

I knew if we stole the children, the parents would follow. Figuratively of course.

Solution

Knowing this much, let's walk through this innovation together. Grab your pen and pad and answer the questions I pose.

I have to lay out all the questions and answers here, but at any time, put the book down and try to guess the next question and the answer to that question on your own. You can solve this!

What we know: We need to get to kids.

1. Question: Why kids, again?

Answer: Grab the kids and you have the parents, families, and the schools. Go ahead, write it down.

2. Question: What do kids like to do?

Answer: They like to play.

3. Question: What do kids like to play with?

Answer: Toys.

What we know: I have no budget, so I can't advertise.

4. Question: What communication media do I have that doesn't cost anything?

Answer: The Internet.

What we know: Toys need to be tangible.

5. Question: What is the only device connected to the Internet / computer that can take something from the Internet and make it tangible?

Answer: The Printer.

Here's the big reveal: I need to create a tangible toy for kids to play with that can be distributed over the Internet!

Why Kids? = Families, Schools, Camps, Day Cares, etc...
What Do Kids Like To Do? Kids Like To Play...
What Do Kids Like To Play With? Kids Play With Toys...
Only Marketing Medium? The Internet...
Only "Tangible" Tool? The Printer...
Solution...
Create A Tangible Toy For Kids To Play With
That Can Be Distributed Over The Internet!

When I developed the final product, I realized its potential as a corporate specialty advertising tool. My first pitch was to United Airlines. Here's how it went.

> "What if I could create a specialty advertising product similar to a tea-shirt or coffee mug, with your marketing message and logo, which we can change every 15 minutes, where your customers, who will represent all demographics, men, women, and children, rich & poor, across all cultures and ages will actually ask for it, and I'll handle the manufacture and fulfillment anywhere in the world, 24 / 7 / 365, instantly, and each time I fulfill one it will only cost you 10¢. Are you interested??

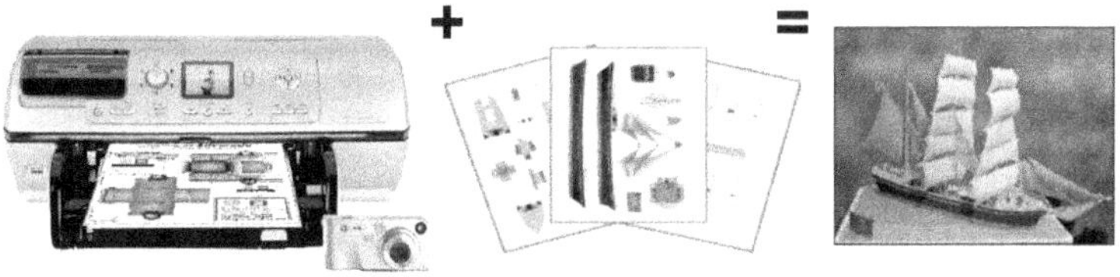

Our first product was this.

After the first month, United contacted me to re-negotiate. They said that even at 10¢ each, they didn't have a budget for the 750,000 people who came to their website.

Since then, I have completed contracts with British Airways, General Motors, The City of San Diego, the Department of the Interior, Kia, and more. The store now has over 100 products that cater to teachers, parents, school kids and their projects.

I have three U.S. Patents on the concept and have had more than 45,000 customers and generated more than $1 million!
The company is called Paper Models, Inc. and can be found at www.PaperModelsOnline.com. Here, you can download nearly 50 free paper models.

What started out as a fun project to increase the awareness of the Port of San Diego, turned into a company that provides fun for kids and parents, instant school projects, and corporate specialty give-aways.

The purpose of this chapter was to give you simple examples of how you can learn to ask the right questions, arrive at the correct answers, and develop ideas that can help you in your daily life or actually become a company.

You Can Do It!

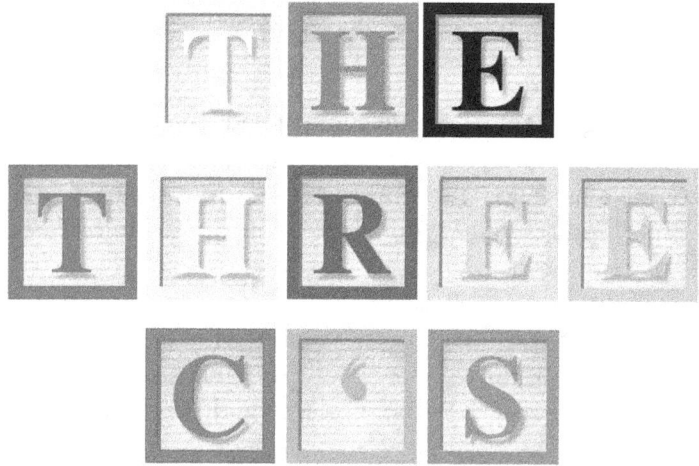

CHAPTER 10

THE THREE C's

Chapter 10

The Three C's Of Innovative Thinking

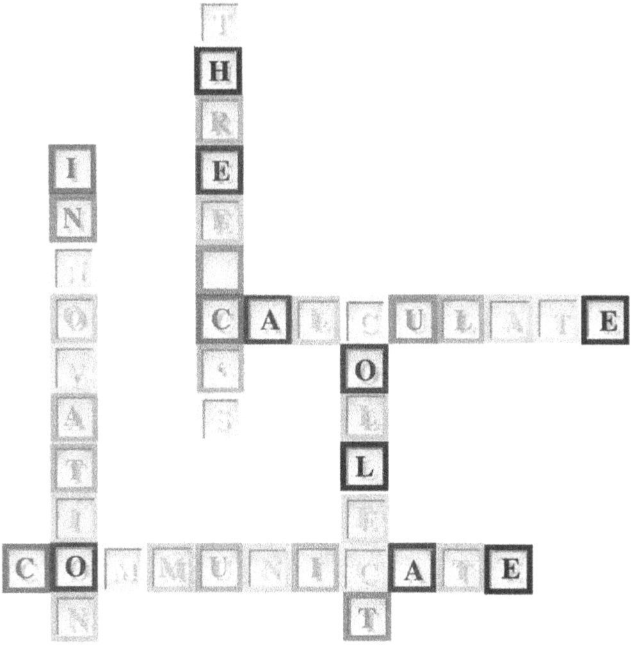

In this chapter, we get down to business with an an actual formula to help you solve problems on a daily basis. The Three C's of Innovative Thinking was the result of nearly three years of analyzing the process, I instinctually used to solve problems. It was difficult to identify because I just did it. It's like riding a bike? After a while, you just do it.

In the years of research, since I discovered this process, others have attempted to identify how the human brain thinks creatively. What surprised me was the Ph.D.'s, scientists, and geniuses, who describe their process turns out to be the same. While the names of the individual components differ, the process works the same.

Here's how the creativity process works.

The innovative thinking process is a function of three components, Collect, Calculate, and Communicate.

1. Collect

2. Calculate

3. Communicate

Let's break each one of these down and see how they work.

"It is not enough to just do your best or work hard. You must know what to work on. "
-W. Edwards Deming

Steven Wright • The Alphabet

http://bit.ly/2jDwovO

COLLECT

Collect

We have discussed the "Collection" part of the Three C's throughout the book. As discussed previously, look around, gather data, just keep collecting information from as many different places and industries as possible.

You probably won't recognize what's important and what's not until your "creative" brain starts to put the random pieces together. The random pieces could be something you saw today or something you remembered from childhood. It is most always, random.

I like to read Discover Magazine. This science magazine has amazing articles on nearly every discipline. You can search the web in a random fashion or randomly view YouTube videos. I may start out watching videos about innovation, then end up watching videos about time travelers. Who knows where it will take you. Go with the flow.

Often your subconscious will direct you. It may know which direction you should go even though you have no idea at all.

Take Notice

Science professor Guy Claxton once observed "Creative people are expert noticers. They have highly developed abilities for visual foraging; spotting, gathering, and utilizing things that most others overlook. Having an active rather than idle curiosity about the world around you reveals ideas. Be nosy, be "eyesy."

Be "eyesy!"

"Thinking well is wise: planning well, wiser: doing well, wisest and best of all."
-Persian Proverb

Baader-Meinhof Phenomenon

Most of us have experienced the Baader-Meinhof Phenomenon, more than once in our lives. This is where we come across a random name, image, number, color, make, or model, that is unfamiliar to us, but then you see the same thing over and over again.

It's like when you buy a new purse, you then see lots of people carrying them. Or, you buy a new car then you often see the same car on the road.

Sometimes we call this "vuja de". It's the opposite of deja vu. We all have experienced deja vu, where you're experiencing for the first time, but you think you've experienced it before. Vuja de is when you look at something you have seen many times before then all of a sudden it's as if you are seeing it fo the first time.

There's no telling how long or how quick the collection process will take. Sometimes it can take a long time, maybe months, depending upon the magnitude of the problem you are trying to solve. More often, it's instantaneous, because your innovative brain makes a random connection with something you already have experienced and remembered.

I can promise you, the more your practice what we are discussing, the quicker this collection stage will happen then the faster answers will come to you.

"Concentration is my motto - first honesty, then industry, then concentration."
-Andrew Carnegie

The Five W's

To help the collection process, there are a few things that will help. Be proactive in researching random topics. You'll know it when you see it. You can also take a close look at the problem or innovation you are trying to solve. Remember, not all innovation is to solve a problem. Sometimes it's just for fun or to create something new. Angry Birds wasn't to solve a problem other than getting Rovio' rich.

The closer you look at what you already know, the easier it will be for your subconscious to find the missing pieces. One very powerful technique is the Five W's; Who, What, Where, When, Why, and How. I guess it should be called the Five W's and an extra H, but that doesn't sound as good.

The Who, What, Where, When, Why, How techniques have been attributed to Sakichi Toyoda, the founder of Toyota. Sakichi found great success using this in the 1970's to propel Toyota into the major league of auto manufacturing. But sadly, he didn't invent it.

The Five W's was first used in the late 1800's and early 1900's by The New York Times. The Times wanted fresh news from inside all of the densely populated ethnic neighborhoods. Neighborhoods they could send reporters into.

So they would find young boys; 12 years old or so and turn them into reporters (Cub Reporters, get it? "Cub" reporters). They were told to go get the stories and if they answered the Five W's, they would have enough information. Then a real reporter could turn the information into a real story. For each story they got paid 5¢.

The point being, if you thoroughly answer the Five W's, you will have told the story about your problem, what you know, and what you don't know well enough. Your subconscious will then identify what's missing and how to solve your problem.

Let's take a closer look at the Five W's.

Here's a quick example using the Five W's on the Paper Models Marketing Campaign from above.

Who: The "Who" was, who did the problem affect?

As mentioned above, it actually affected the Port of San Diego. As the Port is common to all of the W's, let's take that out of the equation. When I analyzed it closely, the actual affected parties were children, parents, and teachers. We weren't reaching them.

What: The "What" was, determine and identify exactly what is causing the challenge or the problem.

The problem was marketing to children and parents without a budget. We had to hook the kids (and the parents) some way. If we hooked the kids, the parents and teachers would follow.

Where: The "Where" was exactly where does the problem happen? Where does the solution need to be applied?

As we determined above, we didn't have a budget to work with, so it had to be free so, I chose the Internet.

Why: The Why was why does the problem occur? Why is it happening? We aren't reaching our complete demographic, the kids, parents, and teachers. These individuals are a huge influential market segment.

When: The when was, when does it happen. When do the kids NOT engage when they should. It turned out it was 24/7/365, especially on nights and weekends.

How: The How was, how am I going to hook kids for free over the Internet. The answer fell out… Downloadable toys and educational school projects.

I know, I would never have pitched it this way to my boss at the time. It sounds way too creepy, but you know what I mean.

"If you really want something you can figure out how to make it happen."
-Cher

The Seven Why's

Here's another fun technique for getting to the bottom of things. It's also really fast. It called The "Seven Whys" of problem solving.

There's no question who invented this technique. Anyone who has had or has ever been around pre-schoolers know the Seven Whys parent torture.

You've heard it before.

Child says, "Mommy, why is the sky blue?"

Mom says, "Because of the water in the air."

Child says "Mommy, why is there water in the air?"

Mom says, "Because the sun evaporates the water and it goes into the sky."

Child says, "Why doe the water evaporate Mommy?"

Mom, "Because the sun heats up the water… Enough!"

That's as far as I remember from my childhood. I usually got hit about now.

Here's a practical Seven Why's question / answer scenario. Watch how the continuous series of "why" questions lead you to a solution.

Problem: I can't start my motorcycle… Why?

Answer: There's no charge in the battery… Why?

Answer: My alternator didn't charge it… Why?

Answer: My alternator belt broke… Why?

Answer: Because I never checked it for wear… Why?

Answer: I never created a checklist… Why?

Answer: I never took the time… I don't know, maybe I should.

Conclusion: Is the time to create a checklist less time and effort than the time and effort to fix the belt and recharge the battery?

It's now your turn. Think of a recent problem you've encountered and go through the seven whys to see if it can bring any clarity to the problem and a possible solution.

Try it!

"It is not enough to have a good mind, the main thing is to use it well."
-Rene Descartes

CALCULATE

Calculate

Calculate is the easiest part of this three part formula. This is the part where you just kick back and wait for it to happen.

During this time, you will still be Collecting and matching the new information with the information that is already in your subconscious. It's like assembling a puzzle. Your brain keeps the pieces that fit together and sets aside the ones that don't until the puzzle is complete.

The Calculate phase of this formula has a wide range of time necessary for this puzzle building to happen. For me, it has happened as quickly as in an instant and sometimes it has taken up to nine months. Here's an example of the nine month time frame.

Swimming Pool Aerator

I lived just outside of Phoenix, Arizona on and off for 20 years. If you've ever been to Phoenix, you know you always have to have water nearby. You need water to drink and to cool off, especially in the summer. Most people who live there have swimming pools in their backyards.

In most of the country, people want their pools to get warmer earlier in the swim season and stay warmer later in the year, but not in Phoenix. Every pool has something called Aerators. They are pipes connected to the return water flow on the swimming pool pumps that when are switched on, spray the water up to 10 feet in the air in a big fan shape.

We turn these aerators on and run our pool pumps at night when the air temperate is cooler, the exchange heat from the pool water into the air to cool the pool. It's difficult to believe that an entire in-ground swimming pool could get so warn by the sun that it's actually uncomfortable to swim in.

Well, one day, the pipe leading to the aerator spray nozzle broke inside the Cool-Deck patio. Cool-Deck is a type of concrete and texture that is a little bit cooler when you walk on it with bare feet than standard smooth concrete. It's also more expensive and difficult the patch because of the texture.

With the broken pipe embedded in the concrete, there was no way around jack-hammering the entire concrete deck, replacing the pipe, re-pouring the concrete deck, and adding the Cool-Deck texture. It about killed me to jack-hammer out a perfectly good patio for a 99¢ piece of PVC pipe.

So, I thought I'd give my Three C's a try. It was the end of the swim season and I had some time before I needed to make a decision. I looked around on line, I looked at the home improvement centers, I looked at outdoor magazines, but nothing came to mind.

Suddenly, nine months later, Eureka! I got it!

I realized that if I bought a $3.47 masonry circular saw blade and simply cut the existing expansion joint about a 1/4" wider, I could press a new PVC pipe down into the joint and reconnect the new pipe with the existing pipe in the soil at the back edge of the patio. All I needed to do then, was to fill the opening with a tube of $4.98 concrete joint filler.

Instead of the project costing me $3,000 and having the concrete texture and color never match, it cost me $8.45 and 30 minutes of my time.

It was a good thing I wasn't in a rush. I just put this problem on auto-pilot and waited for the solution.

"Genius is one percent inspiration, and ninety-nine percent perspiration."
-Thomas Edison

COMMUNICATE

Maya Angelou called this her "Piddling Time".

Steven Wright • Afraid Of Heights

http://bit.ly/2zTbi0G

Communicate

The Communicate phase of this formula is by far the most important. This is where you have to allow and provide an environment where your subconscious right brain can communicate with your conscious left brain. This part is extremely easy to do if you are willing to allow. Just give yourself an environment of quiet. The nearly impossible part of this task is to give yourself an environment of quiet. Seriously.

When teaching top executives from around the world. I challenge them to do this on the way home from the Masterclass. I tell them this is a homework assignment. An assignment I am going to check on in the morning. The task is only NOT turn on their radio or iPhones, or any noise producing device from the hotel to their homes and back again in the morning. They all smile at me. They're thinking to themselves, "This is easy, I can do that!".

The very first item of the following morning is to ask them, by a show of hands, who completed the homework assignment. Out of every class of say 100, 2, maybe three completed this assignment.

This tells me the difficulty in turning off the phone, to remove the mental clutter and distraction from their lives. We all need to just spend some quality time with ourselves. If you got to know yourself a little better, you might just like who you meet?

And, you will definitely learn new things about yourself and most likely have a flood of ideas you just couldn't hear with all the background distraction. I think you know what I am going to ask you again to do.

TURN OFF YOUR PHONE. You or no one else with die. The President will not call you. Your company will not shut down. Trust me! There is not one thing your phone will distract you with over the next 30 minutes that is more important than becoming more innovative!

Interruptions Are Destructive

In The Zone

Have you heard the expression, "Being in the zone?" Have you ever been in the zone? If so, you know exactly what it means. It means you are so focused that you are one with your thoughts, your game, your performance.

If during this time, you were told to "take a break", "walk it off", or "Honey, can you look at the disposal?" the zone disappears. It's gone. Luckily, it's not gone for good. You can get back into the zone, maybe. It often takes 30 minutes or so to get into your creative or high performance state of mind. And, that's if you can. Many times you are bumped "out of the zone", it's gone for the time being.

If you want to be consistently creative and innovative, you need to set a given amount of time and place set aside where you can focus without interruption. Interruptions are completely destructive to creativity. Some people can deal with disruptions, while most others are stopped dead in their tracks.

You must avoid interruptions from the outside as well as from yourself. The BIGGEST pitfall and distraction is YOU! Subconsciously, you are much more comfortable doing things you know you can succeed at rather than something you might fail doing. You are never sure if you can get into the zone and if you do, will you come up with that next David, 5th Symphony, of Mona Lisa? Most of the time, we don't.

We have a tendency to focus on things we like to do and things we are comfortable with. Don't: answer email or even touch your phone. Leave your dog alone. They will be fine for an hour. Don't feed your fish, organize your paperclips, file your folders, trim your nails, check your text messages, and by all means… Stay away from YouTube! YouTube is great in the Collect mode but is a killer in the Communicate mode.

Some people can play music in the background, most can't. If you try, be sure to start with "Relaxation" "Meditation", or New Age" music. Rap ain't going to do it for you. Any music with a strong driving beat and often lyrics, will kidnap your left brain and force it to perform manual labor. It will have to keep the beat and sing the lyrics along to the music and never allow your right brain a chance to communicate.

As I said earlier, the Three C's have been called by other names. Some scientists add or delete a step here and there, but this seems to be the best, most focused formula for innovative thinking.

If you follow these three rules, I promise, you will become more creative.

I bet as you go through this book, you are already seeing new ideas pop into your head. It will happen while walking, exercising, taking a shower, or driving to and from work with your radio off. I am sure you are already getting new ideas!

This book is far from over, but I want to remind you to come on over to my website at www.Safko.com. Hit the "Contact" menu and share your ideas and the environment you were in when you got these innovative ideas. Also, share the frequency of getting creative ideas. I will bet the frequency is increasing as well.

Lose Your "Need For Noise"

"The time to repair the roof is when the sun is shining."
-John F. Kennedy

20 Ways To Eliminate Stress Without Leaving Your Desk

The Communicate part of the Three C's can also be a form of meditation. Meditation is nothing more than focusing your mind and shielding yourself from outside disturbances. When you can eliminate outside interference, you bring your body and your mind to a calm state. It's only in this calm state that your right brain can Communicate to your left.

Often, we are required to be innovative at work. Finding your calm space can be really difficult. I have a "spinner" and an egg of Silly Putty on my desk near my keyboard at all times. I get it at the .99¢ store. I also keep Silly Putty in the console of my car. It's great for when you are stuck in traffic. Here are 20 ways to help eliminate stress without leaving your desk

- Ipad your stress away
- Play Solitaire
- Pictures of the family (Unless you have a family like mine.)
- Deep breathing / meditate
- Affirmations
- Calisthenics
- Jokes
- Youtube
- Silly Putty
- Scooby Snacks (Citrus, Vitamin C)
- Write (journal, blog, comment on others)
- Power naps - 20 minutes works wonders
- Doodle
- Call your family (see above)
- Surf the Web (set time limits, though)
- Coloring
- Build a puzzle
- Sing Out Loud (quietly)
- Read (children's books, poetry, comics, or a cheesy magazine)

"The doctor can bury his mistakes but an architect can only advise his clients to plant vines."
-Frank Lloyd Wright

20 Ways to Eliminate Stress By Leaving Your Desk

- Go to the park
- Play a video game
- Watch an animated kids movie (like "Sing")
- Visit a playground and ride a swing
- Go to the zoo
- Go roller skating
- Buy a coloring book & color
- Create & eat your own recipes
- Read a bunch of random greeting cards
- Go to the mall people watch
- Get an Etch-a-sketch or Rubik's Cube
- Play hide-n-go seek
- Play Candyland or Twister
- Go skipping
- Take a walk
- Sing in public
- Write a poem
- Go to the beach
- Watch the clouds
- Read something unfamiliar

"The best time for planning a book is while you're doing the dishes."
-Agatha Christie

Steven Wright • Dry Ice

http://bit.ly/2mFfVZc

When I ran my computer company, we would often take the day off and go hiking in the desert. We were always surprised how many amazing ideas we got while walking and climbing. It was a completely different environment, free from stress. It was always a very creative place to be.

One day I was totally stressed out so, I got in my car and drove from Phoenix to Tucson where This Old House was filming an episode. I always enjoyed the show, Norm, and the gang. It turned out I had an amazing day on set and went home rejuvenated.

Above is Norm Abram, Lon Safko (me), & Steve Thomas
This Old House.

"It was a beautiful little Theory, murdered by a gang of brutal Facts."
Charles Lamb

I will Guess Your Card

Here's a fun little card trick I can actually put on the pages of this book.

I will guess your card. Here is how we will do this. I will place 5 cards face up below. I want you to study the cards and pick one card out. Don't tell me the card. Just focus on it. Keep focusing on it. Don't tell me the card.

Now that you have picked your card, I will think about you thinking about it for a while. I will read your brain waves, and remove your card from the lineup.

Look on the next page and be amazed!

Did I remove your card?

When you figure this trick out, send me an email to **lon@Safko.com** and tell me how it was accomplished.

If you can't figure out how the trick was done, look at the last page of the book for the solution.

Think Differently

Coloring Outside Of The Lines

About a decade ago, our granddaughter of 8 was coming to stay with us for spring break. If you or anyone you have ever known who has had the responsibility of entertaining an 8 year old for more than an hour, you know the fear my wife and I had anticipating her arrival.

In preparation, my wife to Wally-World and bought a big box of Crayons, and a half dozen coloring and activity books. We were certain that hundreds of activity pages would keep her busy for an hour at least.

On the second morning, she asked if she could color a picture for me. I said, yes that it was very important to me and that should take her time (giggle), and make it extra special. And when she was done, if it turned out great, I would put it up on our refrigerator for the world to see!

(Where or when did they pass that law that all children's works of art must be immediately posted to the nearest refrigerator?)

Her and I carefully went through all the coloring books, selecting possible candidates and eliminating non-contenders, until we hit on one. We chose the Desert Tortoise.

She cleared the table, carefully aligned every color crayon, took a deep sigh and was about to begin coloring her masterpiece when I said. "Sweetheart, this is very important to me, I want you to do something different. I want you to color 'outside' of the lines."

She looked up at me as if I said I had grown another nose. What? she asked. Yep, color outside of the lines.

I said that for two reasons. I was always trying to teach them to question everything and not just follow convention. The second reason was, I had NO idea how anyone could color outside of the lines! I wanted to see what happened.

About this time, my wife gave me a dirty look as I was always screwing with the grandkids heads. She knew if I had a round room, I would tell them to go sit in the corner. I wanted to see what it took for smoke to come out of their ears.

She agreed and I left her to her to her work. After 20 minutes or so, I knew the joke was on me. She had completed the coloring and it was freaking amazing! She had taken the brightest colors in the box, and outlined the shapes with the colors she would have normally filled in. The bright colors adjacent to the black lines and white background made the image vibrate. It was almost iridescent!

The image below, is unfortunately, not hers and unless you bought the Premium Color paperback, it's not in color. Her masterpiece remained on our fridge for months until it got dog-eared and discolored and had to be retired to the recycle bin. (After she was long gone back home of course.)

Sometimes the masterpiece is hidden right in front of you if only you can look at everything differently. You need to look outside of the box and color outside of the lines.

Wayne Dyer once said, "If you change the way you look at things, the things you look at will change."

I tried to reproduce her work of art on the computer, but could only approximate her genius. She actually colored outside of the lines and it was great!

"There are nights when the wolves are silent and only the moon howls."
-George Carlin

Innovation - The Food Wheel

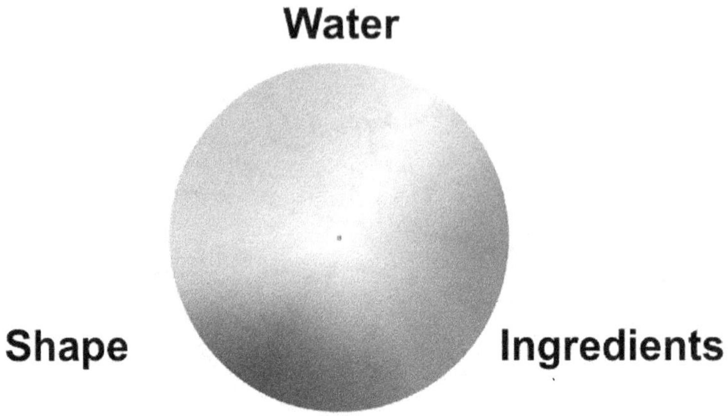

Here's another innovation realization I came up with several years ago while sneaking a Taco Bell bean burrito; The Food Wheel. What if…

What if you looked at all recipes as basically the same, but where only the shape and quantity varies. Here's an example.

Let's start with a typical chicken dinner. The dinner consists of chicken (meat), potatoes or rice, (starch), a steamed vegetable (vegetable - duh), and a glass of water.
Now, let's take the chicken off the bone and cut it into large pieces, cut up the potatoes into large pieces, and throw the meat, starch, and veggies into a pot with half the glass of water. You have Chicken Stew.

Let's do that again. Cut the chicken smaller, use the rice for the starch, throw in the veggies, and now add the full glass of water.

You have Chicken Soup!
One more time… Put the water back on the side, keep the chicken in large pieces, change the veggie to lettuce and tomatoes, and change the starch to bread. Throw a little mayo into the mix and you have a great Chicken Sandwich!

Pretty weird, right?

As I said earlier, I was inspired (inspiritu), while sitting in a Taco Bell when I noticed the "BRILLIANCE"! Taco Bell's entire menu (for the most part), is made up of only five ingredients; tortilla, meat, cheese, beans, & lettuce.

Sometimes the tortilla is fried and crunchy as with a taco, sometimes if soft as with a burrito. Sometimes the meat is chicken, but it's mostly beef (which I think is mostly beef?)

Next time you are in a Taco Bell, look at their menu and think of the Food Wheel!

Your Food Wheel Recipe

Here's a couple of activities for you. Grab your pad again…

1. Write down at least three recipes that change only by varying the meat, starch, veggie, and water.

Come by my website www.Safko.com, select contact and let me know what you've come up with!

2. What kind of soup would you eat for dessert?

Write down at least one recipe for a dessert soup.

I'm thinking black cherries marinated in a cherry liqueur covered with a heavy cream with a dark chocolate liquid, and slivered dark chocolate on top, served warm… OMG!

"We ought to spend more time "wondering" than "doubting whether." Wondering is the key to progress."
-Gerald Horton Bath

Steven Wright • Tarot Cards

http://bit.ly/2hIzvSJ

CHAPTER 11

TECHNIQUES

Chapter 11

Techniques

Brainstorming - How do you brainstorm ideas?

Brainstorming is a problem solving technique using rapid generation of ideas. In a group, everyone is encouraged to toss out ideas as quickly as they enter their minds. The more spontaneous contribution of ideas from all members of the group, the better.

No value judgments, just an outpouring of ideas. All concepts and ideas are welcome. This creates a safe environment and a synergy, with one idea spurring another.

Do this until the ideas are exhausted. Then, analyze what you have learned as a group to determine which ideas are helpful in solving the issue at hand.

"Art is as natural as sunshine and as vital as nourishment."
-MaryAnn F. Kohl

Mind Mapping

Mind Mapping is similar to brainstorming except ideas are visually expressed on a white-board or flip charts by topic area. As with Brainstorming, you start with your core idea and write it in the middle.

The team then starts naming ideas that need to be considered regarding that first concept. Then you build further and further out until you have visually mapped out all of the related topics.

The last part of mind mapping is taking a break, then re-look at what you have developed to eliminate ideas, rearrange ideas, and add new ones.

Check out the new on line mind mapping collaboration tool Coggle at www.coggle.it

The Octopus Chart

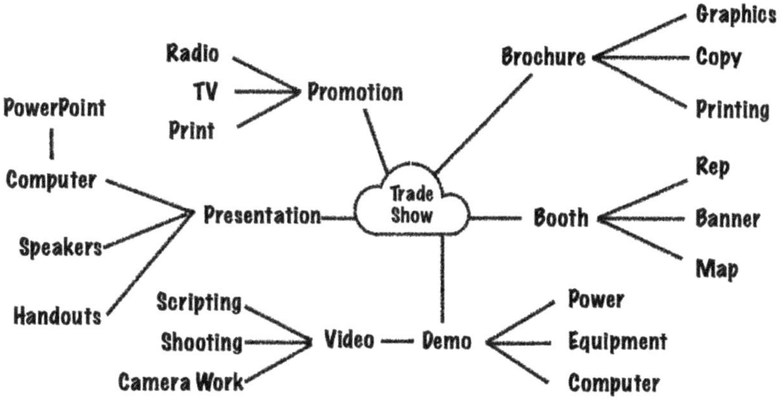

Dr. Seuss wrote Green Eggs & Ham when his editor challenged him to write an entire book using less than 50 different words.

SWOT Analysis

SWOT Analysis, the old standby. It's an oldie but a goodie.

It really is a good way of positioning your idea in the bigger picture.

You start by creating the following four heading. Then, as a group, you list everything you can about your concept that fits into each category. If you spend enough time on this, a very accurate picture of your problem / solution will emerge giving you very insightful ideas.

Strengths **(Internal)**	***Weaknesses*** **(Internal)**
Opportunities **(External)**	***Threats*** **(External)**

"Creativity is allowing yourself to make mistakes. Art is knowing which ones to keep."
-Scott Adams

Divergent vs. Convergent Thinking

We are going to take a look at many different techniques scientists and innovative thinkers have found to help them develop their creative thinking ability.

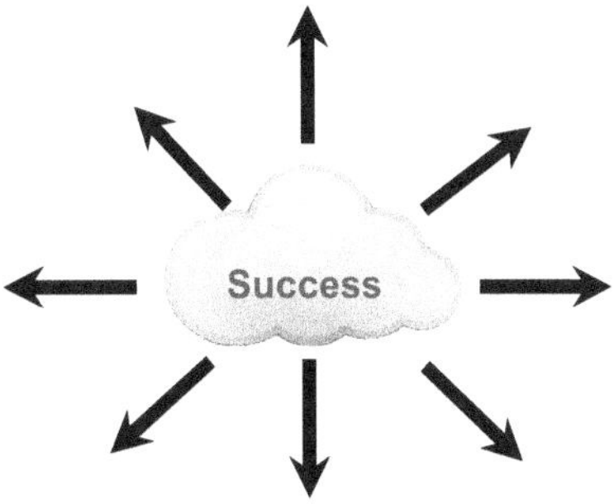

Some techniques work much better for some than for others.

We are going to start with Divergent versus Convergent Thinking. This is the yin / yang of looking at solving a problem. Divergent Thinking or question asking is open ended and asks the question "What don't we know?" Where Convergent Thinking makes the statement "This is what we know so far."

Some examples of Divergent questioning would be; "What might success look like?" or "What criteria can we use to measure that success?"

Examples of Convergent are; "Here's the best idea we have so far." and "These are the best criteria to accurately evaluate success."

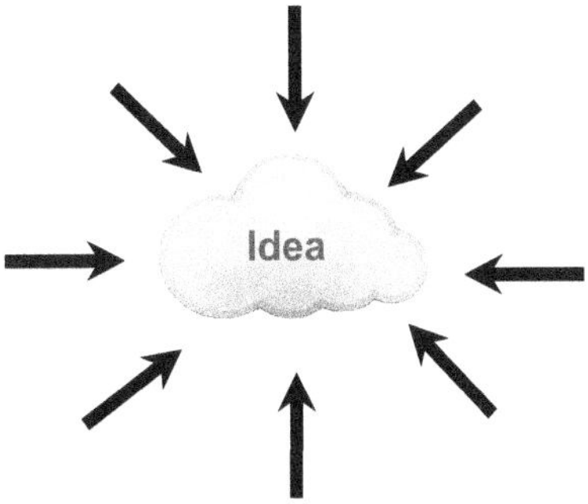

It is important to look at your starting point (and steps along the way, in these two different perspectives. You never know which one will yield the best insights. It's fast and easy, so start here.

"The quickest way to double your money is to fold it and put it back in your pocket."
-Will Rogers

Try This Now

Time for another activity! Grab your pen and paper.

Take a few moments and write down an example of a problem.

Write that problem down both ways, Divergent and Convergent. Here is an example for each.

Divergently, e.g.: How can we get women to become repeat customers?

Convergently, e.g.: We need women to become repeat customers.

Your turn:

Divergently: ________________________________

Convergently: _______________________________

Stop Asking Questions That Result In Yes Or No

It really bothers me when I hear someone ask "You don't carry these, do you?" :o| Ask open ended questions like:

"In what ways can we reach new segments of the market?"
"How can we increase our response rates?"
"How can we increase our customer retention levels to 98%?"
"In what ways can we complete our projects on time and on budget?"

"Think left and think right and think low and think high. Oh, the thinks you can think up if only you try."
-Dr. Seuss

Steven Wright • Instant Coffee

http://bit.ly/2jBr0cH

What Is The Hidden Parking Space Number

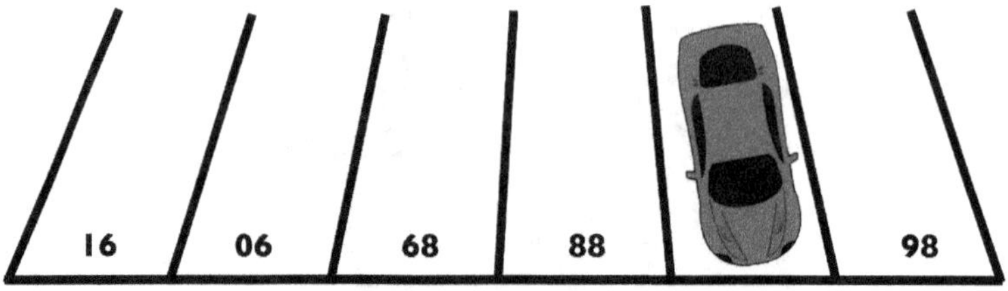

Think differently. The answer is on the next page.

"Have no fear of perfection, you'll never reach it."
-Salvador Dali

SCAMPER

The idea analysis technique called SCAMPER was invented by Bob Eberle, and popularized in books like "Thinkertoys". It's a great acronym that allows you to easily remember how to see your ideas from a completely different perspective. SCAMPER stands for:

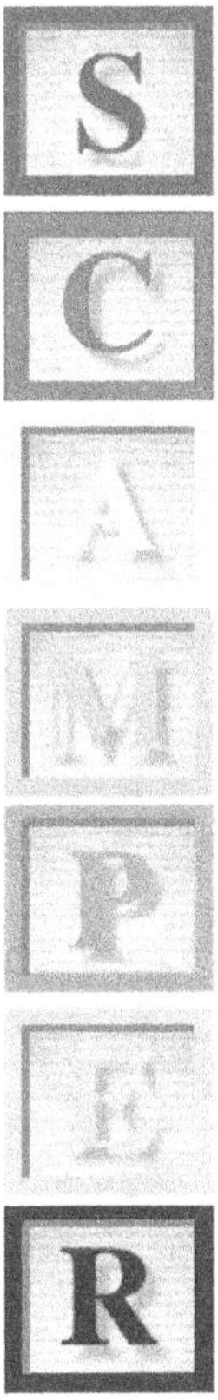

Substitute

Combine

Adapt

Modify

Put To Other Uses

Eliminate

Reverse / Rearrange

Oh yeah, the answer to the previous parking space problem is…

87

SCAMPER is an activity is where you choose a particular topic and develop it through a structured process. The following is taken form MindTools: http://bit.ly/2Bnc7iS

Substitute

- What materials or resources can you substitute or swap to improve the product?
- What other product or process could you use?
- What rules could you substitute?
- Can you use this product somewhere else, or as a substitute for something else?
- What will happen if you change your feelings or attitude toward this product?

Combine

- What would happen if you combined this product with another, to create something new?
- What if you combined purposes or objectives?
- What could you combine to maximize the uses of this product?
- How could you combine talent and resources to create a new approach to this product?

Adapt

- How could you adapt or readjust this product to serve another purpose or use?
- What else is the product like?
- Who or what could you emulate to adapt this product?
- What else is like your product?
- What other context could you put your product into?
- What other products or ideas could you use for inspiration?

Modify

- How could you change the shape, look, or feel of your product?
- What could you add to modify this product?
- What could you emphasize or highlight to create more value?
- What element of this product could you strengthen to create something new?

Put to Another Use

- Can you use this product somewhere else, perhaps in another industry?
- Who else could use this product?
- How would this product behave differently in another setting?
- Could you recycle the waste from this product to make something new?

Eliminate

- How could you streamline or simplify this product?
- What features, parts, or rules could you eliminate?
- What could you understate or tone down?
- How could you make it smaller, faster, lighter, or more fun?
- What would happen if you took away part of this product? What would you have in its place?

Reverse

- What would happen if you reversed this process or sequenced things differently?
- What if you try to do the exact opposite of what you're trying to do now?
- What components could you substitute to change the order of this product?
- What roles could you reverse or swap?
- How could you reorganize this product?

Begin With The End In Mind

Steven Covey teaches us in "The Seven Habits Of Highly Effective People", you need to visualize the end result then work backward. Lay out the specific steps you need to take until you get to the beginning.

It's similar to what Michelangelo said about creating his masterpiece, David when he said: "I just chipped away everything that wasn't David."

Michelangelo already had an image of the end product, what David was to look like upon its completion. He had such a vivid image of the finished David, that he really did just chip away, down to where David was hidden.

Often, when I build something like a round collapsable table or an Adirondack Chair, I see the finish vision of what it will look like, I then identify every piece it takes to create the table or chair. At that point, all I have to do is cut the pieces to match the image in my head and assemble it.

When you use this to change the direction of your life or to focus on a very large project, we often use what is called a Dream-Board or Vision-Board.

I want to share another personal example of a solution to a problem I had in 2002 that set my life on a course I could never have foreseen. Vision Boards or Visualizing The End Really does work. Here's how.

In 2001 I decided even though I had been speaking professionally on and off since the mid-eighties, I wanted to speak full time.

I contacted a friend of mine who owned one of the top 10 most successful speakers bureaus in the U.S. I asked him what I needed to do to become a professional speaker. He mentioned a bio, one-sheet, press photos, etc., but stressed that all successful speakers need a book. I had never written a book before and didn't know the first thing about being an author.

I had written 12 short stories for fun since college and had them on my computer. I gathered them up, edited them, and put them into two books "Gratuitous Serendipity" and "Life Is But A Dream" (both on Amazon), and self-publish. Self publishing was new and a big deal in the early 2000's.

After I achieved this feat, I contacted my friend and told him of my success. I didn't have one book published, I had two!

He told me he didn't want to burst my bubble, but he meant "legitimately" published, published by a publishing house, a real publisher, not self-published. Needless to say, I was nearly devastated. I knew getting a "real" publisher to publisher your book had less of a chance than getting struck by lightning.

I know you've heard the saying before, getting struck by lightning, but I truly would have bet on the lightning. I had no idea how I was going to accomplish this.

I was a strong believer in focus. Focus on the end product and you will automatically find a way to get from here to there. As I said earlier, I used this concept for building furniture.

I decided what the… Heck. I set out to create a book cover. A pretend book cover of a legitimately published book by a real publisher. Here is the cover.

It was a back cover of a book about how I developed the First Computer To Save A Human Life and the struggle of constantly being ripped off by Apple, IBM, and Microsoft, investors, and the inevitable lawsuits. I created a title, image, book outline, and even took the time to scan an ISBN barcode from another book just to make it look as real as possible.

I have to look back and laugh. The website at the bottom of the cover said "www.TheRightPublisher.com". This masterpiece made it to my refrigerator door. As I said early, all children's art must be placed on a refrigerator door immediately.

It hung there for several weeks when... I was speaking with a friend of mine who was a prolific serials author. He had published 14 business books through several "real" publishers.

During our conversation, I walked to the kitchen to get more coffee and turned to the fridge for the milk. As I reached for the handle, I saw my fake book cover and knowing who I was speaking with I asked "Hey Frank, I have an idea for a book. Do you think you can introduce me to your publisher?" He said "Sure! Why not!".

The idea I had for the publisher wasn't for "When You Walk Among Giants". It was something I had been noticing for the past year. When I had the opportunity to pitch the publisher, I told them that we were entering the biggest residential home construction phase in human history. She laughed and asked for a marketing plan and said she'd take it to "Blue-Sky", the meeting they have to determine whether or not they want to publish the book.

I submitted the proposal and they accepted my book. That was 2004 and the book was published by Pearson Publishing. in 2005. The book was called "Build Your New House In No Time, How To Work With Contractors". Do you remember what happened to home building in 2005 through 2009?

Bingo! It worked!

I would never have thought to ask my friend about an introduction if it weren't for the book cover being on my fridge and reminding me of my unsurmountable goal.

Vision-Boards work. Create one for yourself. Get pictures from a magazine or the Internet, glue them to some foam-core, cardboard, cork-board, or hang them on your refrigerator.

Build An Innovative Network

Innovative by association. If you want to be more innovative and originate unusual ideas, then surround yourself with people who are innovative as well. Get creative and inspiring people into your social circle and interact with them on a regular basis.

I had a partner for 17 years who when we got together to think of new ideas, products, and companies, we joked that "We could feel the magic!". And, he was right. When out-of-the-box thinkers get together and are in the zone, there is a kind of magic and a proliferation of great ideas.

Companies and trade associations often take advantage of this magic by creating "Think Tanks". A Think Tank is a great way to generate new ideas, especially using the techniques outlined above.

If you can't participate in a Think Tank, bounce your ideas off other creative people. Whenever I get what I think is a creative idea, I first ask my wife. She's been part of our think tank for three decades. She has a great mind to determine what will sell, what won't, and how to sell.

Listening to fresh perspectives and seeing your issues in different angles may help you construct your ideas. The re-focus will help you substantiate the problem and narrow down solutions.

Several of the people in my Think Tank network are Pat Sullivan who invented ACT CRM software, Gary Witt, Ph.D. in Psychological Marketing, Sam Wise, the co-inventor of artificial reality and the inventor of the Data-Glove, Gary Thuerk, the sender of the First SPAM Email Message, and Vint Cerf, the inventor of the Internet. Feel that magic!

"The chief enemy of creativity is 'good' sense."
-Pablo Picasso

The Paper Airplane Challenge

The Paper Airplane Challenge is great to do with a group, but might not be as much fun if you are sitting quietly somewhere by yourself holding your Kindle.

Many of the activities above can be and are designed to be group activities and I have modified them so you the reader could still perform them.

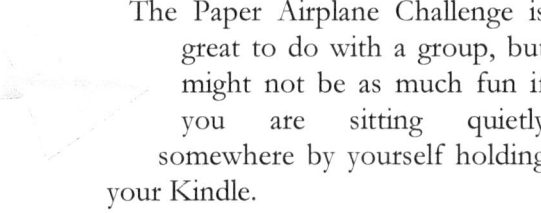

This activity works great as a group activity, but you can still do the activity by yourself. While it might not be as much fun, the core lesson is still there and I strongly encourage you to participate. Remember, you will get out of this book, only what you put into it. Here goes.

You are challenged to build the best paper airplane possible. It will be judged not by looks, only by how far it flies.

RULES (Group)

Use one sheet of paper, 3 minutes to discuss the design, and 5 minutes to build it. Then we fly!

If you are performing this activity by yourself, I recommend that you try to make at least three different paper airplane designs. Here, you are competing against yourself and your own ability to create an award winning paper airplane by strictly adhering to the rules.

When you or the others at your table are ready, we can launch. Find a large area where when you throw your airplane, it can fly as far as the design will allow without obstruction.

Have someone keep track which plane flies the farthest. If it is just you, it will be very easy.

For the group, you will have a clear winner. For yourself, which design worked best? Was it your first idea? The one you always build? Or, was it a new design. Did you push your own limits and look for different ways to get it to fly farther? I hope you did. It's this pushing yourself that will return the highest rewards. It's like exercising any muscle… No pain, no gain.

What if you took the original design for your plane and came up with three improvements and tested them to see if it made a difference?

A Lesson For flying Outside The Box

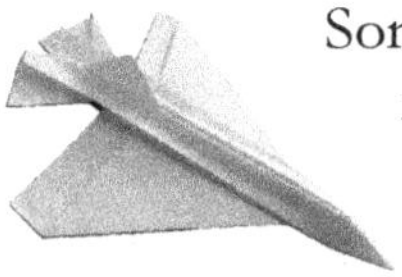

Some of the creative solutions are really outside of the box. I love it!

One person took all of the airplanes from the group at the table, rubber banded them together to increase their weight (mass) so the had more momentum.

One group found an office chair with wheels, placed the airplane on the chair and kicked the chair across the finish line! Very innovative!

My all time favorite solution didn't come from my Masterclass, it came from a book I read about 10 years ago. The book was called "Paper Airplane, A Lesson for Flying Outside Of the Box".

This was another easy to read, 30 sentence book, with mostly all illustrations about a child with autism participating in a class airplane contest.

SPOILER ALERT!

If you don't want to know how the book ends, quickly skip the next page.

The story describes the frustration of a young boy participating in a school wide competition for the furthest flying paper airplane. and how he was being partnered with a classmate who has autism.

The boy continually pushed his partner for ideas, designs, trail tests of the models, but the autistic boy just didn't interact. The boy becomes more and more frustrated and angry as they approach the deadline for the flight contest.

As the boy stood in line in the school's gymnasium watching all of the other teams flying their most innovative designs, he noticed the autistic boy was only holding one flat sheet of paper. No design, no creativity, no way to win. The boy became really angry and decided to fly his own plane and leave the autistic partner behind. The line moved forward the boy became increasing more confident he made the right decision to leave the other boy on his own.

When it came time for the boy to fly his design. He stepped up to the flight line and threw his best shot. The plane flew. It flew well. It didn't win. The boy lost but felt he at least had a shot at the contest.

The autistic boy was last to fly his design. He stepped up to the flight line with his single flat sheet of paper, looked around, and balled the paper into a tight ball. He took a deep breath and threw the paper ball overhand as hard as he could.

The ball bounced off the wall on the other side of the gym. The autistic boy won the competition. Why?

Because he followed the rules. The same rules I provide above. The rules never said it had to look like an airplane. It only said, "Use one sheet of paper, 3 minutes to discuss the design, and 5 minutes to build it."

So, why didn't you think of that? You didn't think of that again, because of conditioning. There are dozens of blocks that prevent us from thinking creatively.

1. Believing you aren't creative
2. Making assumptions
3. Making up rules (blocks) that don't exist
4. Following the rules too strictly
5. Being too serious
6. Peer pressure
7. Avoiding risks or afraid of being wrong
8. Always staying with your routines / habits / comfort zone
9. Thinking there is only one solution
10. Making judgments too quickly

Now, add your own!
11. ____
12. ____
13. ____
14. ____
15. ____

Do you see the pattern in the book yet? Break out of your conditioning and think differently.

"Imagination rules the world"
– Napoleon Bonaparte

Popular Mechanics Paper Airplane

If you really get into designing, building and flying paper airplanes, here's what Popular Mechanics considers one of the best designs ever!

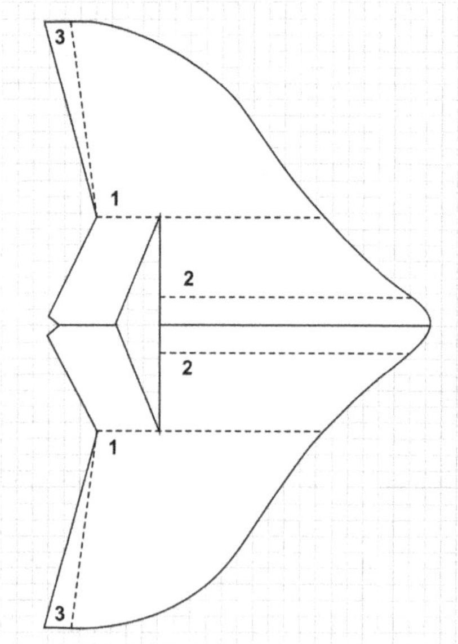

http://bit.ly/2zo7Mev

Transform Problems Into Positive Action Statements

Turn your statements into positive statements. Always use double positives in a sentence whenever possible.

As an example, I really dislike it when someone says "Don't hesitate to call!" Let's look at this statement. Read the word aloud and you tell me your first feeling about that word.

"DON'T". How does that word make you feel? How about "HESITATE". Does that make you feel any better?

How about "Please feel free to call me at any time." Do you walk away with a different feeling? Try these.

"Yes, we are number #3 and we can be #2 in 12 months!"

"Yes we are smaller than our competitor and we can create lucrative niche markets better than they can.".

Do you remember the Ivory Soap story? It wasn't 56/100 percent contaminated. It was 99 and 44/100 percent pure!

Do you remember the Avis Car Rental slogan in the 60's?

AVIS®

We're number two, we try harder.

(In P.R., we call that "Spin".)

"Always drink upstream from the herd."
-Will Rogers

Embrace Absurdity

Absurdity is the inspiration of some of the most creative ideas of the 19th 20th centuries. Edward Lear and Lewis Carroll used absurdity in storytelling. Can you name the books? From the Marx Brothers to Monty Python, comedians have counted on absurdity as a source of comedy for hundreds of years. Frank Zappa used it for his music, and The Dadaists such as Salvador Dali, and other surrealists used it to create absurd, but amazing art.

The funniest comedy and the most innovative ideas are the ones where you put together, two seemingly related ideas. Ideas that at first seem to go together, but exactly how isn't apparent.

Here a couple of personal examples. I hope you don't tire of these. My plan is that you can learn how easy it is to perform them. If I can do it, anyone can!

I was watching David Letterman's opening monologue in the fall of 1999. At that time, the news was filled with only two items, El Niño and the movie blockbuster, Titanic.

El Niño is, of course, the wet cold counterpart to the warm dry La Niña 15 year weather cycles that comes off the Pacific Ocean. It was the first time meteorologists used the term to describe the terrible flooding the U.S. was experiencing in the mid-west. And, of course, the movie Titanic was breaking records at the box office and was to take home 11 Academy Awards.

Letterman started with a couple of good jokes. Then says "They found out today, the Titanic was actually sunk by El Niño!" This was really funny and absurd. He took the two largest news items of the day and mashed them together. We knew El Niño cause problems, we knew the Titanic sunk, so why put the two together?

Why not, because it's absurd. How could a weather phenomena in the Pacific cause the sinking of an unsinkable ship in 1914?

When you gave it some serious thought, you immediately found the humor in that statement. I thought what if?

I knew it was only meant to be funny. I know that's how humor works. But, what if it were true?

The following morning I hit Google early and hit it hard. I found NOAA (National Oceanic and Atmospheric Administration) website and found a web page a complete list of data on El Niño / La Niña cycles for the entire 20th century.

What do you think it showed for the spring of 1914? We were right in the middle of one of the largest El Niño cycles that had occurred in a hundred years. As Captain Smith was retiring as a sea captain on the maiden voyage of the Titanic, he had probably only sailed the North Atlantic for 20+ years. The El Niño / La Niña cycles are 15. His experience could have only been one El Niño cycle which was a mild one.

His lack of experience with the El Niño cycles which could melt glaciers and drop an inordinate amount of icebergs in the North Atlantic in April. Captain Smith would never have expected the amount of ice that far south for that time of year. He was piloting the Titanic based on his entire career's experience. The result…

El Niño DID Sink The Titanic! Who knew? If you want to read the story it is in my book "Gratuitous Serendipity" on Amazon, but because you bought this book, here it is for free: **http://bit.ly/2A2qFY3**

Steven Wright • Button Hole

http://bit.ly/2j4Tc3I

Microwaved Candy Bars

An engineer Percy Spencer was working with magnetrons electronic devices in 1945. Magnetrons were developed to send microwave radio signals.

As Percy Spencer stood next to a functioning magnetron, he felt the chocolate bar in his shirt pocket suddenly soften to a gooey consistency.

He deduced that the microwaves emanating from the magnetron had melted his chocolate bar. He realized that he found a way to heat food by using radio waves. He also realized that if he could heat food, he could also cook food.

This serendipitous insight led to the invention of the microwave ovens we use today.

"We don't make mistakes, just happy little accidents. "
-Bob Ross

The Absurdity Continues

Here are a few absurd questions I asked myself over the year and returned some astounding surprises.

- **1978:** What if you could get a computer to speak to you?
- **1985:** What if you spoke to a computer and it did what you asked?
- **1986:** What if you could control a mouse just by moving your head?
- **1986:** What if you could sipped on a straw and could turn on a light?
- **1987:** What if you could click buttons and have the computer speak for you?
- **1987**: What if you could puff on a straw and control a hospital bed?
- **1999:** What if you could send virtual toys over the internet?

Don't be afraid to ask bizarre, unexpected questions, you just might be surprised at the answers!

What They Did During World War II

Cadillac:	Made tanks.
Bulova:	Made Torpedo Mechanisms.
Brunswick:	Made assault boots.
Trane AC:	Made intercoolers for planes.
Caterpillar:	Made engines for M4 tanks.
Whirlpool:	Made Propellers.

Look At Everything Differently.

"Creativity is intelligence having fun."
-Albert Einstein

Edison Talking Doll

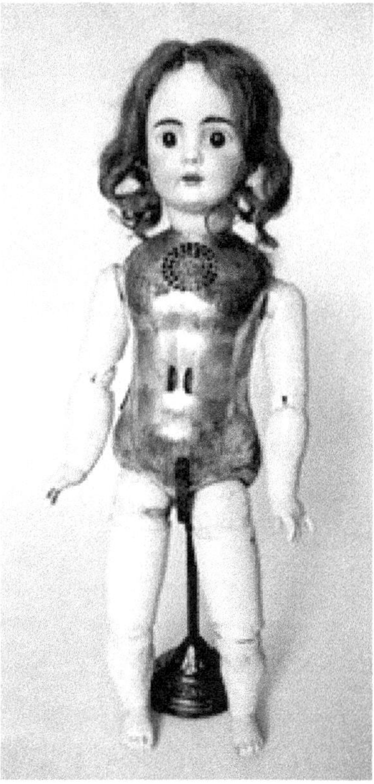

Did you know Thomas Edison, the inventor of the lightbulb and the first to illuminate Wall Street also invented the first talking doll?

The doll said the poem "Twinkle, Twinkle Little Star". The little girl's voice was recorded in the fall of 1888 on a metal cylinder that played back at 80 RPMs.

It is currently owned by the National Park Service, collection (EDIS 1279)

If you want to hear the doll speak, here is the link to the recording. If you think the doll is creepy, wait until you hear it speak!

This thing would give Chucky nightmares!

http://bit.ly/2A1c2nH

"Creativity requires the courage to let go of certainties."
-Erich Fromm

No Sleep

Time for another activity. Grab your trusty pad and pen.

What are three ways the world would be different if people didn't needed to sleep?

What would you do with the extra time?

Write down at least three ideas for each.

Write down three industries that might be impacted if no one ever had to sleep again.

"The best way to have a good idea is to have a lot of ideas."
-Linus Pauling

Follow These Directions

Don't put your pad and pen away yet!

Here's 10 questions. Look at each and write the answer on the pad. Don't read the answer at the bottom of the page.

1. Pick a number between, say, 2 and 9
2. Multiply that number by 9
3. Add the first digit and second of that number
4. Subtract 5 from that number
5. Write down the corresponding letter of the alphabet
6. Write down the name of a country that starts with that letter
7. Write down that last letter of that country's name
8. Write down an animal that starts with that letter
9. Write down the last letter of that animal's name
10. Write down a color that starts with tat letter.

Now, let me ask you.

"How many Orange Kangaroos do you think there are in Denmark?"

Think Differently - Repositioning

Keep your pad at hand.

Take the company you work for and describe their product as if it were a:

Movie ______________________________

Vehicle ______________________________

Love Letter ______________________________

If you don't have a company or product use the iPhone.

How would you describe an iPhone as it were a movie or a vehicle or a love letter?

This should make you think a bit. Just give me two paragraphs for each.

"If I had an hour to solve a problem I'd spend 55 minutes thinking about the problem and 5 minutes thinking about solutions."
-Albert Einstein

Random Association - Wikipedia

Finding random ideas, believe it or not, can sometimes be difficult. We always seem to look in the same place.

Here's a tip to find truly random ideas.

Wikipedia. At times the articles are helpful and other times they are just nonsense. If the article makes no sense, click it again. You will find what you're looking for.

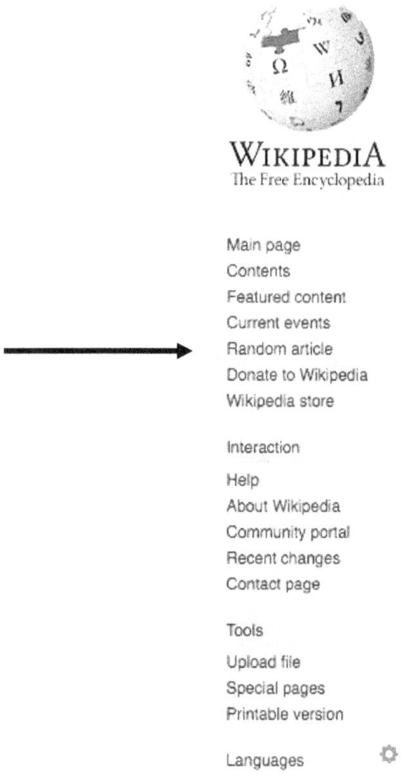

"You can learn more about a person in an hour of play than you can from a lifetime of conversation."
-Plato

Associative Innovation Or Random Association – Smart Phone

Here's another random association. Who would have thought by combining the functions of a laptop into a cell phone would be a good idea… Steve Jobs, that's who.

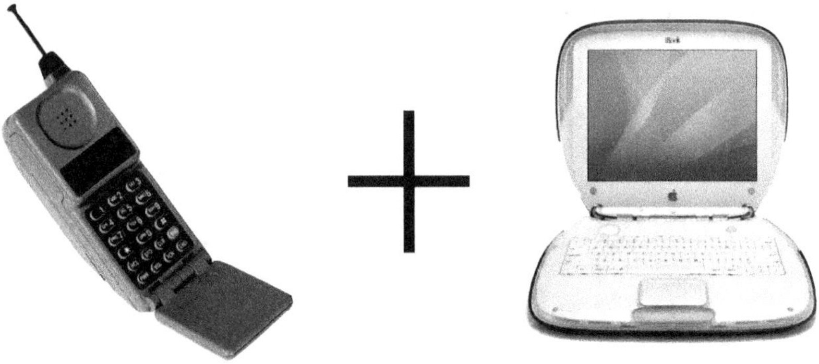

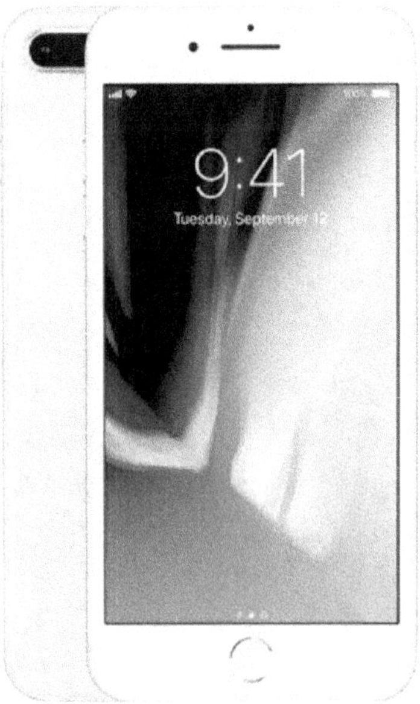

Steven Wright • Coffee Table

http://bit.ly/2zegEGD

Random Association – Movie Totles

6 Movie Titles

Here's another activity. Use your pad and writing device and write down six of your favorite movie titles.

Titles

____

____

____

____

____

____

Now, choose any two of the titles, then combine the plots.

Write down a couple of paragraphs about the plot for your new movie.

And, try to do the first one in under 3 minutes.

Were you able to do it?

"Creativity is contagious. Pass it on. "
-Albert Einstein

Random Association – Connect The Words

Let's try putting some random words together to see what kinds of creativity sparks it can generate. Grab your paper and pen and get writing.

Develop a list of 20 random words. The first words that come to your mind. (Also, fun to do as a group).

1. ________________
2. ________________
3. ________________
4. ________________
5. ________________
6. ________________
7. ________________
8. ________________
9. ________________
10. ________________
11. ________________
12. ________________
13. ________________
14. ________________
15. ________________
16. ________________
17. ________________
18. ________________
19. ________________
20. ________________

Now… Let's put two of them together to see what comes up.

Draw a line between a word in the first column to a word in the second column. Find anything exciting?

Steven Wright • Microwave Fireplace

http://bit.ly/2hKEjab

Random Association – Word Asscoiation

This time you get three words. It will be your job to read the three words and write down a word that has the three previous words in common.

The first one is an example.

	Call	Pay	Line	Phone
1.	End	Burning	Blue	________
2.	Man	Hot	Sure	________
3.	Stick	Hair	Ball	________
4.	Blue	Cake	Cottage	________
5.	Man	Wheel	High	________
6.	Motion	Poke	Down	________
7.	Line	Birthday	Surprise	________
8.	Wood	Liquor	Luck	________
9.	House	Village	Golf	________
10.	Plan	Show	Walker	________
11.	Key	Wall	Precious	________
12.	Bell	Iron	Tender	________
13.	Water	Pen	Soda	________
14.	Base	Snow	Dance	________
15.	Steady	Kart	Slow	________
16.	Up	Book	Charge	________

The answers are below. How many did you get?

1. Book
2. Fire
3. Pin
4. Cheese
5. Chair
6. Slow
7. Party
8. Hard
9. Green
10. Floor
11. Stone
12. Bar
13. Fountain
14. Ball
15. Go
16. Cover

Random Association - Alexa Innovation

I love these kinds of random associations. People crack me up.

You have to see these two videos. They are great!

http://bit.ly/2AqZpkY

"Discovery consists of looking at the same thing as everyone else and thinking something different"
–Albert Szent-Gyorgyi

Random Association - Alexa Yorick

http://bit.ly/2jOx6mt

CHAPTER 12

TEAM THINK

Chapter 12

Team Think

Team Meeting Enthusiasm

Let's start this section off with a couple of fun videos which will exemplify how most people feel about meeting and working in teams. The first is a short video of about office meetings the second is one on training seminars. They prove the points.

http://bit.ly/2iMM9Az

Training Class Enthusiasm

http://bit.ly/2ntkyGb

"Good judgment comes from experience, and a lot of that comes from bad judgment."
-Will Rogers

Working on innovation and creativity with a team can return multiples of rewards providing the team has good chemistry. A badly organized Team Think is more than a waste of time. It is damaging.

Any collection of individuals will work. The trick is to have a good Team Think leader. A leader who can identify the other members strengths and weaknesses. The environment must be free from criticism and foster fellowship where everyone feels comfortable. A great team leader is very rare.

Let me further express my enthusiasm for a well defined team. Here's an example. Let's say you are working with a team. Let's further say the team consists of 10 members ranging in age between 25 and 55. Let's again assume that the average age of the entire team is 40.

Then, by definition you have brought together 10 members times 40 average years, 400 years of human experiences to solve your problem. Every person on that team comes from a different background and culture, education and life experiences, economic and geographic.

All 400 years of experience represent totally different perspectives. And, as we have learned from the previous discussion, different perspectives mean different information and different ways of solving the same problem. Respect the use of teams, respect your team members, and figure out how to lead them to greatness.

"A mind stretched to a new idea, never returns to its original dimension."
–Oliver Wendell Homes

Lessons From Geese

As each bird flaps it's wings, it creates an uplift for others behind them. There is 71% more flying range by flying in a V-formation than flying alone.

Lesson 1: People who share a common direction and sense of common purpose can get there quicker. Whenever a goose flies out of formation, it quickly feels the drag and tries to get back in position.

Lesson 2: It's harder to do something alone than together. When the lead goose gets tired, it rotates back into the formation and another goose flies at the head.

Lesson 3: Shared leadership and interdependence give us each a chance to lead as well as opportunities to rest. The geese in formation honk from behind to encourage those in front to keep up their speed.

Lesson 4: We need to make sure our honking is encouraging and not discouraging. When a goose gets sick or wounded and falls, two geese fall out and stay with it until it revives or dies. They then catch up and join another flock.

Lesson 5: Stand by your colleagues in difficult times as well as in good.

Jack Eberenz, The Franchise King

Finding the Essence

Here are some examples of how large corporations help their employees successfully work in teams.

At Cambridge Technology Partners, a software development firm, there are four rules for fast teams:

1. Let groups make their own rules. Teams must be in charge of their own destiny.

2. Speak up early and often. If a team member has a problem that they can't solve within two minutes or less, they need to ask for help.

3. Learn as you go. Conduct regular review sessions to determine what worked, what was learned, and what needs improvement.

4. Fast has to be fun. People can burn out quickly if they are constantly under the gun. Plan weekly outings to reenergize staff. Teams function better when they get to know each other in different settings outside of work. It benefits the team and benefits the organization.

Hallmark Cards of Kansas City developed a "creativity center" stocked with clay, paint, paper and other art materials to help the creative staff "think with their hands." Hallmark employees are energized by the freedom to create.

The typical workweek at Longaberger Company, a maker of handcrafted items, is 35 hours long. There is an unwritten rule that up to a quarter of each workday should be spent having fun. Employees are energized because they know management trusts them to have fun and get the job done.

And, you all have heard the stories about Apple Computer in the 1980's and Google today. I have been to both and the stories are true.

Steven Wright • Raisin Wine

http://bit.ly/2zQpcTI

Participative & Energetic Meeting

Here are a few tips to get you started with your next innovative team to ensure a more participative and energetic meeting.

- Hold the meeting at a time (prior to break or lunch) and in an environment conducive to communication.

- Keep the meeting brief.

- Be well prepared in advance for even a shorter meeting.

- Have a clear agenda so you and the team know what your purpose is for scheduling the meeting.

- Make sure you achieve the purpose.

- Take notes during the meeting so you can follow up on what was discussed with appropriate action plans.

- Make sure the topics are work or group-related. Don't deviate.

- Be honest and straightforward. Remember, you're the authority.

- Back up whatever you say with facts. If you make a promise, follow up on it.

- Set aside time for discussion, but limit questions by requesting that they be held until you are through talking.

- Schedule no more than five or 10 minutes for questions. Offer to answer any remaining questions after the meeting on a one-on-one basis.

- Keep your tone positive and supportive.

- Make the meeting livelier by planning the unexpected. Nothing is more boring than routine.

Pull Together — Win Together

Follow these rules to set your team up for success:

- Define each personas roles.
- Draw up a game plan and be sure everyone knows what it is.
- Create an identity for the team. *
- Be willing to reassign roles, responsibilities, and positions.
- Give your members a chance to stretch their skills & responsibilities.
- Continuously reinforce the team concept.
- Encourage networking and working together.

The key to establishing and maintaining good teamwork is to create a caring atmosphere. If employees believe in their leader truly cares about them, high performance will naturally follow.

We've previously discussed what happened at Apple when Steve Jobs took Apples' 21 best engineers and moved into the house behind the headquarters to develop the Mac. Talk about building a team identity!

"Never confuse movement with action."
–Ernest Hemingway

Steven Wright • Science Fiction

http://bit.ly/2AREhB8

Houston… We Have A Problem

An Example Of Lateral Thinking

Here's a great example of "Lateral Thinking' and how NASA solve the oxygen problem onboard the Apollo 13 space capsule.

http://bit.ly/2A3pesm

Lunar Survival

This is a GREAT activity which shows the power of team.s It was developed by NASA in the 1960's but it's amazing how it proves that two heads (or more) are better than one. I always use it whenever I train groups to work on teams.

If you are reading this book. then most likely you are alone and not surrounded by team members or NASA. So a) you will have to trust me on this and b) use it the next time you have the opportunity to work on or with a team.

Here is the NASA scenario:

You are a member of a space crew scheduled to rendezvous with the mother ship on the lighted surface of the moon; however, due to mechanical problems, your ship was forced to emergency land 200 miles from the scheduled rendezvous point.

During reentry and landing, much of the equipment aboard was damaged. Your survival depends on reaching the mother ship 200 miles across the lunar terrain.

After taking careful inventory of the items not damaged, you find that 15 items are left intact and undamaged.

Your job is to rank your inventory in terms of their importance of how each will assist you and your crew to to reach the rendezvous point.

Place the number 1 alongside the most important item, the number 2 next to the second most important and so on. The number 15 will indicate the least important item for your Lunar Survival.

Grab you pad and pen and let's get cracking. Time is running out.

Lunar Survival Inventory

You will need to seriously think about each and every item. You can't or don't need to try to carry everything. You will need to be able to justify every item you choose. Think about why you would take it or why you would leave it.

_____ Compass, magnetic

_____ First aid kit w/ hypodermic needles

_____ Flares, signal

_____ FM receiver/transmitter (solar-powered)

_____ Food concentrate

_____ Heating unit, portable

_____ Map (stellar map, moon's constellations)

_____ Matches (1 box)

_____ Milk (1 case dehydrated milk)

_____ Oxygen (2 50kg tanks)

_____ Parachute silk

_____ Pistols (2 .45 caliber)

_____ Raft, Life (automatic inflating)

_____ Rope, Nylon (20 meters)

_____ Water (25 liters)

Lunar Survival Scoresheet

When working this activity with your team, you will need to print out this scoresheet to compare how your choices measured up to the team choice and how they measured up to the NASA experts.

If you are performing this activity by yourself, just compare the expert's answers to your own. The most important part of this exercise is "why" are your answers different. What did the NASA team think of that you missed?

I know the image is small and trying to look at it on a Kindle or an iPad will drive you crazy every time you turn the tablet to look at it in landscape view and the tablet changed the view making it sideways again.

I will put this scorecard and other information I wasn't able to put in this book on my website. Just go to www.Safko.com, select "Free Content Access" and I will send you a password to access all the free content in this book.

Lunar Survival Ranking of Inventory By NASA Experts

Here's how the NASA Team ranked the 15 inventory items based on importance for survival.

Oxygen	1	Fills respiration requirements.
Water	2	Replenishes loss by sweating, etc.
Map	3	One of the principal means of finding directions.
Food Concentrate	4	Supply daily food required.
FM Receiver	5	Distress signal transmitter, possible communication with mothership.
Rope	6	Useful for tying inured together and help in climbing.
First Aid Kit	7	Oral pills or injection medicine.
Parachute	8	Shelter against sun's rays.
Raft	9	Along with CO canisters for self propulsion across chasms, etc.
Flares	10	Distress call in line of sight.
Pistols	11	Self propulsion devices.
Milk	12	Mix with food for nourishment..
Heating Unit	13	Useful only if landed on dark side.
Compass	14	Very weak magnetized poles, therefore useless.
Matches	15	With no oxygen, little or no use.

How did you compare? Did you find that the wisdom of the crowds might have increased your chances of survival? Did you see that maybe by bringing hundreds of years of experiences and perspectives returns more innovative results?

Team Think Is Critical

Team Think is one of the best ways to encourage employees to motivate themselves and one another to develop innovative solutions.

Remember, everything we discussed in this book thus far which applied to you personally to get you into condition for creative thinking, also applies to each individual team member. Here are some highlights that will remind you how to get your team thinking creatively.

- ✦ Know your team members and their individual goals.
- ✦ Give them permission to be participating members of the team. No judgment.
- ✦ Include, don't exclude. Encourage them to participate.
- ✦ Create opportunities for them to express their thoughts, ideas, and opinions in a caring neutral environment.
- ✦ Value the individual and their input.
- ✦ Encourage them to listen and give feedback to one another.
- ✦ Communicate all information to the team.
- ✦ Encourage team member to improve the processes.
- ✦ Give employees permission to say "yes" to ideas they think are good.
- ✦ Break down barriers by encouraging team building skills as a core competency.
- ✦ Ask employees from many different levels, what they think needs to be changed and what is working well.

"Creativity comes from a conflict of ideas."
-Donatella Versace

CHAPTER 13

MOTIVATION

Chapter 13

Negative Reinforcement

Negative reinforcement can drain the spirit of your Team Think the same way as it drains your creativity. Avoid hidden pitfalls when looking for ways to offer support and guidance to your team.

What results would you expect from a Team Think that is driven by a culture of negative reinforcement?

Here are four indications that Negative Reinforcement is present:

1. Does productivity go up just before the deadline?

2. Does performance decline dramatically after reaching a goal or milestone?

3. Does performance drop after removing a performance goal.

4. Do team members use "negative talk."

Always remember, there is a high price to pay for negative reinforcement.

Here are the major de-motivators:

Boredom	Daydreaming
Procrastination	No Skill Enhancement
Fatigue	Accidents
Quality Suffers	"Just Get It Done" Mindset
Dissatisfaction	Rumors
Turnover	Low Morale

"Man is only great when he acts from passion."
-Benjamin Disraeli, 19th century British Prime Minister

What Motivates You?

In order to be creative, you need to be motivated. There are many things that motivate different people.

From my experience, engineers are motivated mostly by success. Success in the form of "I did it!" When I owned my software company and 30 employees, it was surprising how different each person's motivations were.

The software and electrical engineers were motivated by making it work. The admin staff was motivated by "organization." The sales team by far was motivated by money.

Money isn't a bad motivator. It's easily measured. It was more quantitative and less qualitative. It is much easier to develop programs to motivate salespeople than engineers.

When you look at your own innovation, you need to consider what motivates you. Is it fame? Do you want to be famous for creating the next killer app? Is it just because you can? Or, is it money, wealth that motivates you.

For me, the difficulty with innovation was always understanding my motivation. For decades I never worried about money. It never motivated me. I built the computer systems for the disabled first, because I really got excited when I was able to help someone. My second motivation was because I could. Building something no else had before then seeing it work, really motivated me.

While helping people and doing things no one else has done before as they say, doesn't pay the bills. Until I realize that for innovation to survive, the innovator needs to survive. It took about 20 years for me to understand this and slightly shift the way I looked at the rewards for innovation. I slowly included compensation to my motivation mix.

Now that I have motivation in balance, I can innovate and not have the stress of financial worries which would otherwise destroy my ability to innovate.
Grab your pen and pad and turn on your brain (and your emotions). It's time to be honest with yourself. You don't need to show this to anyone and I promise, I won't look.

In a recent survey of several large companies, management was asked what they thought was the top five motivators for their employees. Then, the employees were asked to list their top 5 motivators.

Rank your responses to questions 1 through 5, plus be sure to fill

	Employers	You	Employees
1	Money	________	Appreciation
2	Job security	________	Being an insider
3	Chance for promotion	________	Personal Sympathy
4	Good working conditions	________	Job Security
5	Interesting work	________	Money
	Other	________	

in the "Other" space with your most important motivator.

How different were your answers when compared to a typical employer. What did you write under "Other"? How would you rank that answer when added to the list of all the answers given above?

Remember to keep this in mind when managing your Team Think!

"You may have to fight a battle more than once to win it."
-Margaret Thatcher

Maslow's Hierarchy

I am sure you have seen the Maslow's Hierarchy before. It's real, it applies, and I wanted to remind you of this study to help you understand motivations.

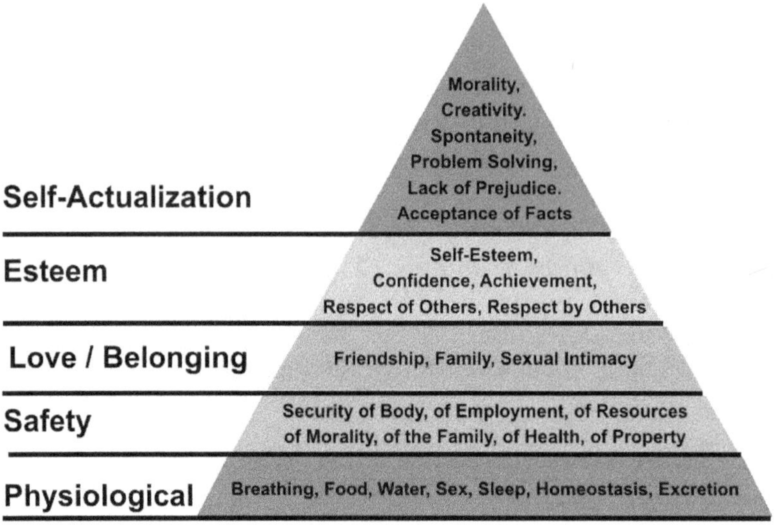

"Only two things are infinite, the universe and human stupidity, and I'm not sure about the former."
- Albert Einstein.

Steven Wright • Sea Shells

http://bit.ly/2j6yLUf

Naysayers & Negaholics

Nothing will drag an innovative team down faster than naysayers and negaholics. Just one of these personalities can kill the creativity of an innovative team in only a few minutes. Management and legal are famous for playing these roles. Remember, it's their job to see what can go wrong first, analyze the risks, then decide whether or not the reward is worth the risk. The big risk is having them destroy your creative environment.

The best way to get naysaying negaholics on board is making them feel a part of the decision-making process. Successful Team Think teams realize the way to get an individual emotionally invested is to foster an open environment that actively solicits the team member's ideas and promptly acknowledges them.

Continuously keep the channels of communication open throughout your team by:

Sharing the big picture. Communicate your vision to your team and reiterate it often. If team members are wrapped up in the details of a project, they may lose sight of the ultimate objective. Keep repeating the reasons you're all in this together. Give the concrete examples of the rewards (motivation); promotions, raises, recognition, etc.

Being generous with information. Let your team members know immediately when plans change, when problems arise, or when any other changes occur that would affect the team.

Defuse the effect of rumors generated by crisis by giving your team members updates often. Don't hoard information.

Get them on board as quickly as possible. Give them praise frequently and criticism sparingly. Make sure you give all team members plenty of positive feedback. Many members complain they only receive feedback from leaders when there's a problem.

Sometimes a team member does need negative feedback. Praise in public; criticize in private. These signals are closely watched by other team members. And, be prepared and encourage negative feedback on yourself and the way you are managing your creative team.

Encourage team member feedback about you. Take time to listen to your member. They probably have expertise in areas you know little about. If they have suggestions for improvements, give them a fair hearing. If you think their ideas are good, give them recognition. Actions speak louder than words.

Be a confidence builder, not a confidence destroyer. "You're doing a good job, don't mess it up" is positive feedback destroyed by the tagline. Simply leave it at "You're doing a good job."

Choose your words wisely grasshopper.

Divergent Thinking

What Can You Do With A Paperclip

This activity was first developed by J.P. Guilford in 1967. Guilford looked at four areas of creativity;

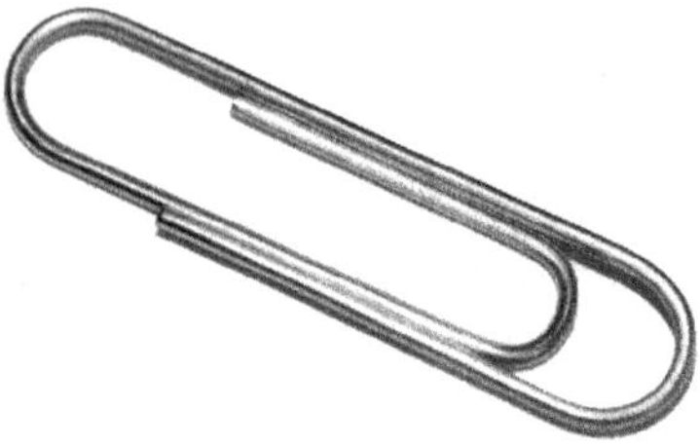

Originality: The novelty of alternative uses for the paperclip.

Fluency: The total number of uses the subject was able to innovate.

Flexibility: The categories with which the alternative uses fell into. And…

Elaboration: The amount of detail the subject provided with regards to the alternative uses for the paperclip.

You can do this alone or as a team activity. If you are working with more than one person, try to break the group into teams. Competition really motivates some people and it's fun to watch.

If you are performing this activity alone, really push yourself to see how many uses you can innovate.

Allow a time limit of three minutes, set the timer, and start the creativity. At the end of the three minutes, rate the teams on each of the categories above on a scale from 1 to 10, except of course, Fluency.

Determine a winner! (Psst…Everyone wins here!)

One Red Paperclip

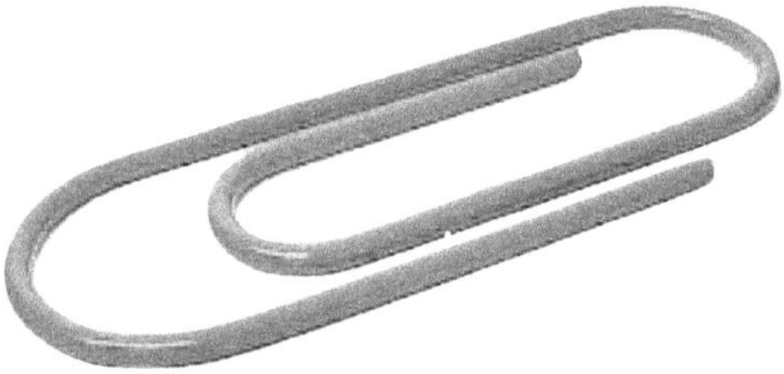

I think this is one of the most innovative individuals and stories ever.

A Canadian blogger named Kyle MacDonald, bartered his way from a single red paperclip to a house in a series of fourteen online trades over the course of a year beginning on July 14, 2005. Here are those 14 trades.

1. On July 14, 2005, he went to Vancouver and traded the paperclip for a fish-shaped pen.

2. He then traded the pen the same day for a hand-sculpted doorknob from Seattle, Washington.

3. July 25, 2005, he traveled to Amherst, Massachusetts to trade doorknob for a Coleman camp stove.

4. September 24, 2005, he went to California and traded the camp stove for a Honda generator.

5. November 16, 2005, he traded the generator for an empty keg, IOU to fill the keg, & neon Budweiser sign.

6. December 8, 2005, he traded the "instant party" to Michel Barrette for a Ski-doo snowmobile.

7. February 2006, he traded the snowmobile for a two-person trip to Yahk, British Columbia.

8. January 7, 2006, he traded the second spot on the Yahk trip for a refrigerated cube van truck.

9. February 22, 2006, he traded the truck for a recording contract with Metalworks in Mississauga, Ontario.

10. April 11, 2006, he traded the recording contract to Jody Gnant for a year's rent in Phoenix, Arizona.

11. April 26, 2006, he traded the one year's rent in Phoenix, Arizona, for one afternoon with Alice Cooper.

12. May 26, 2006, he traded the one afternoon with Alice Cooper for a KISS motorized snow globe.

13. June 2, 2006, he traded the snow globe to Corbin Bernsen for a role in the film *Donna on Demand.*

14. July 5, 2006, he traded the movie role for a two-story farmhouse in Kipling, Saskatchewan.

He traded up from a paperclip to a house! Go Kyle!

"Never slap a man who's chewing tobacco."
-Will Rogers

Steven Wright • 55 MPH

http://bit.ly/2zfxPYy

Reward Ideation

The last topic I want to discuss in this book is rewarding ideation. B.F. Skinner was one of the most influential psychiatrist in developing the foundation for Behaviorism.

Skinner proved how positive reinforcement worked by placing a hungry rat in what he called a Skinner box. The box contained a lever on one side and a hungry rat. As the rat moved within the box, it would accidentally knock the lever. Immediately, a food pellet would drop into a container next to the lever.

The rats learned quickly to go directly to the lever after only a few times of being put in the box. The reward of receiving a food pellet if they pressed the lever would reinforce and train them to press the lever again and again.

Positive reinforcement strengthens a behavior by providing a a reward individual (rats), finds rewarding.

If you want to encourage innovation as a positive behavior, you need to reinforce it with positive reinforcement. Positive reinforcement it is critical to an innovative and creative team.

✦ Understand this motivation and develop a plan ahead of time.

✦ Let the team have time away from the office

✦ Pay an incentive for good ideas.

✦ Give awards at team ceremonies.

If you make it worthwhile to be creative and innovative, people will be.

Conclusion

Wow! Now that was one heck of an innovative journey! As you see, everything available on Innovation and Creativity has been put into this volume. This is why it's called the Innovative Thinking Bible. It's everything worth knowing on the subject.

We have covered a lot of ground. We discussed "Perspective" and how our brains can be fooled to the point we just can't see the solution. We discussed "Organic innovation", which I think is a pretty cool concept and one that infiltrates through every facet of innovative thinking.

Also included was an up front to discussion on "Failure". Not a lot of books would dedicate an entire chapter to failure. As you read, failure is just as much a part of the process to innovative ideas as success. Failure happens more than success and as innovators, need to understand how to identify with it and most importantly, deal with it.

We talked about our brains and how they work. Discussed the difference between our left brain, analytical and or right brain, creative. Then "Innovation and Creativity". Where it comes from, how it works, and how often doesn't work.

There was one chapter called "I Can't Believe It" which showed examples of famous people performing life changing innovations and just how short sighted so many people are about innovation, creativity, and change. You also saw the type of opposition you can face going forward as a more innovative person. Don't be discouraged.

We discussed (a lot) of examples of simple "Random Association" and how by putting simple ideas together can create something entirely new. My wish for this chapter is to show you not only "how" to put disassociated ideas together, but that fact that you can do it! It's not that hard and when you practice, you can do it all of the time!

we then discussed the "Three C's", the actual formula for thinking innovatively. Who knew there was a formula? And, something as powerful and discovering a formula for being more creative, was only three simple steps. As we saw, the difficult part was providing the right environment and training ourselves to stop our "stinkin' thinking".

There were dozens of techniques that have been discovered to help draw out every bit of creative juice you have in you. We looked at everything from Mind Mapping to Brain Storming and From SWOT to The Five W's.

Then we discussed an important topic, Team Think. We seldom think alone without the help and influence of others/ If we are required to get creative at work, it is very likely there will be a team involved.

Thinking with teams is significantly different than trying to think alone. As a matter of fact, I don't recommend you think alone. Creativity seldom happens in a vacuum. As we discussed, when you gather a Team Think together and provide the right environment, you can utilize 100's of years of individual experiences and perspectives. The solutions always develop into more complete, more mature ideas, and they come faster.

Lastly, we discussed "Motivation". You only need to completely understand what motivates you, what drives you. When you know this, you can focus on the motivators in you and find the energy to achieve your goals and accomplish your dream.

And finally part of this chapter, we discussed what motivates others and how important it is to understand what it is so, you can provide motivation to your team and realize bigger and better results.

The overarching purpose of this book is to show you the importance of innovative thinking and the power behind thinking creativity. It doesn't matter if you are a design engineer, a physicist, an artist, a business person, in sales or public relations, a teacher, or in the military. You can be retired, or just beginning your career, thinking more creatively will help you throughout the rest of your life.

Being able to solve problems more efficiently and more quickly will always pay off. And who knows, you might just develop the next Pet Rock!

(If you do, remember me, the one who showed you how…)

I hope we can continue our journey together by connecting with me on Facebook, LinkedIn, and visit my website www.Safko.com.

Thank you for sharing your time over these pages of paper or electrons. I look forward to getting to know you.

Lon Safko

Here is the solution to the "I Will Remove Your Card" trick.

I removed them all. I swapped out all five of the original cards with four new ones. This way, no matter which one you pick, I removed it.

🙃

www.ingramcontent.com/pod-product-compliance
Lightning Source LLC
Chambersburg PA
CBHW071251220526
45468CB00001B/82
9781983939884